Inequality

BOOKS BY
BENJAMIN ROBERT SILL, JR.

Inflation: Worse than Vampires, Zombies or the Plague!

Inequality- Must There Be Blood in the Streets!

Government Economics Gone Wild

Downsizing- Efficiency or Greed?

Observations

Inequality:

Must There Be Blood in the Streets!

Professor Benjamin Robert Sill, Jr., retired

To my beloved wife, Yasmin, and my wonderful children, Brittany and Parker

ABSTRACT

Not only are we in the midst of the greatest wealth transfer from west to east globally, but also we are rapidly becoming more of a two-tiered rich/poor society than at any time in history—and that's saying something when considering the robber baron Gilded Age and the wealth of Egypt, Rome, and even the British Empire.

It sometimes seems as though a lot of people are not bothered by being put upon. In today's world of instant communication the information is there that says the average person is being taken advantage of. How come we all allow our government to continue doing bad things to us? Is it that they don't care or that they don't know how to fight it?

> *How can you honestly think one person is worth $20 million just to "act?" Or the same thing for a sports figure who gets paid to do what we did as kids for fun?*

Who's at fault here? After all, we buy the tickets to see the games, matches, races, concerts, movies, shows, etc., that pay the obscene salaries to "talents." Granted, it's a little farther removed when it comes to the CEOs. Although the shareholders are theoretically the owners of a company, we all know that does not mean anything.

A final note. Please don't think the rich are anything special. Note to the "Blue Bloods" of San Francisco. Did you forget that Daddy was an illiterate miner who came into town, got drunk, and married Mommy, the local prostitute?

Contents

INTRODUCTION

Is there a possibility we are beginning to realize the game of "Rich Man, Poor Man is rigged? That those with great wealth and power will always block the way for the not so rich.

In 2015 we have a Democratic President who predictably is concerned about the growing gap between the rich and the poor. Give him and the Democrats a bone for that one. What seemed to be a temporary situation forty years ago has now taken root and become the norm. There are a few reason for that including, technology automating positions, competition from cheaper overseas workers, an unfair and biased tax system favoring the wealthy, and less union protection. All of which would be legitimate reasons for pay not increasing, but what does that have to do with the widening gap? The automation efficiency results should be evenly distributed to workers, not just top management. Why should management benefit solely from technological advancements probably not even invented by them? Change the tax system to be fairer. If there is a problem with the unions then that's the function the government should step in and provide; and if you can get cheaper workers overseas, why not get cheaper CEOs also?

Because the rich are hoarding a greater percentage of the money, others feel the need to borrow to maintain their lifestyle. Now, no one said they were entitled to that life style, but the rich certainly are not entitled to their extravagant lifestyle either. No one is forcing many people to live beyond their means, but we all know how much fun it is to keep up with the Jones. Two wrongs do not make a right. Besides, in my world the more powerful and greater perpetrator is more responsible.

Even life expectancy increases have not been fair. The rich eat better and have better medical plans Money talks. That means that extending out the retirement age would unfairly punish the poor. These same poor people are more likely to develop and live with chronic diseases. The Affordable Care Act (Obamacare) is supposed to alleviate that and also reduce the costs. Either they die because they don't attend to the problem or they take care of it through government subsidies and live longer.

If you don't have anything why not commit a crime? What the worst that can happen, you go to jail and get food and shelter, or you die and end the misery.

Taking that out to its probable outcome, because the poor and the average are not being represented and are feeling put upon, revolution is a real possibility. Who knows exactly when that final straw breaks? The system feeds on itself and get worse as the rich get richer and richer. They control more and more through their contributions to politicians who then vote in laws that favor the rich. A vicious cycle. Once the fulcrum point has been passed, the race usually ends in violence.

The rich through the power game they play among themselves, drive up prices of real estate, cars, and other items. The poor and average have to either go back to the well for borrowed money to keep up, or they just can't keep up and therefore, are excluded from even dreaming of living in the mansion on the hill. Take away that hope and dream and the above mentioned revolution becomes more of an option.

With the exception of the rare athlete or inventor of something neat, what's called the inter-generational mobility has collapsed also. Children can't get out of poverty as easily anymore. Richard Wilkinson, Professor Emeritus of Social Epidemiology at England's University of Nottingham, quipped: "If Americans want to live the American dream, they should go to Denmark" (Volsky, 2014)

You can't agree to tough policies in order to correct an economic downturn when you have no room to maneuver. With no gas in the tank, the car doesn't go. This means that in addition to all the harm done to the average person, the rich hurt themselves because the economy will eventually stall and maybe not recover.

Globalization

Thomas Friedman wrote a book a few years ago saying the world is flat. What he meant was thanks to technology, capitalism, and the protection by the military of the United States Empire, we all now have the same opportunities. (Friedman, 2005) Barf!

Somewhere buried in the book is the insinuation that we all want the same thing, to get rich. There you go again, back to greed. Only now we all can. It reminds me of the peace dividend we were to get after the fall of the Berlin Wall. You know, because we no longer have to fight the Russians and spend all that money doing so, we will have more money, time and personnel to address the good things in life. Someone forgot to mention that we always find another war to fight because we are human (meaning bullies at heart and mean) and the military industrial complex wants to continue earning big bucks building and selling guns and ammo.

Friedman goes on to say that some people don't want to go along with it. You know, people who believe kindness, consideration, happiness, and religion are more important than money. It started out in the manufacturing sector but has morphed into services now as the ability to go global has pushed U.S. pay rates down to international levels. The Internet, for all its good uses, has devastated white-collar workers in the United States. Let's face it, we are now a seasoned advanced society with all the accompanying bad vices and results therein. What do you do when someone does what you do cheaper and better? They are well-trained and better educated. You cling to the old world for all it's worth, just like the British, or any other empire before them.

Take away all those jobs that used to be performed here, software programming, engineering, designing, legal, accounting, medical, actuarial, consulting, and financial-analysis. That doesn't leave much for now.

I am reminded of the comment that it's a recession when a friend gets laid off but a depression when you do. It has to beg the question of whether or not globalization is a good thing. The answer seems to be, as usual, absolutely, if you are on top. To be fair, globalization seems to be working fine for third world countries developing a middle class. Only problem is, that middle class is replacing ours. So, is your neighbor out of work or are you?

Unfortunately, in a capitalistic society it is a zero sum game, meaning someone has to lose for some else to win. The rich are the ones who own the companies that benefit from lower wages and globalized markets. Hence the huge wage gap.

The divide between rich and poor in the United States has reached levels far beyond that experienced in any other developed nation and beyond anything experienced in this country for nearly 70 years. The income inequality is even greater in China than in the United States. But that's because the workers make so very little there. Similar to the above discussion on depressions versus recessions, I suspect most workers in the United States could care less about what's happening in China if the American is going hungry. I also suspect that we in America are a lot closer to the Chinese standards than we are to the standards of Scandinavia, Japan and Europe. Time will tell whether that income inequality in China will have an effect on us. It does indicate we are not alone in our dilemma. Around 500 million people live in coastal cities in China, where most of the manufacturing is and therefore standards are higher, but there are another 700 million who still live in the countryside and are left behind, just like in the United States. At the moment it is a problem for us, as workers have no bargaining power with management due to those in Asia willing to do the same work for less than one-tenth the cost. "Per capita income in the United States was around $54,000 in 2014 versus 46,000 in 2010, while in China it was $7500 in 2014 and only $4300 in 2010" (WorldBank, 2015) So, the big difference is not between China's industrial workers and those in the

United States, and certainly not between China and the United States' wealthy, but between the poor workers and the capitalists in both countries—and the spread is growing.

It is important to realize that these figures are not personal income numbers. They are GDP divided by the population. Whether that population is adults only, working population only or everyone including children, is never determined or discussed. Along with that unknown is the fact that GDP includes all the diarrhea spewed by the government in the form of spending. So if you are not making these numbers, don't feel left out- they are probably high.

All this means is we're really nothing special that would warrant the huge pay given to management and talent.

Factory Workers and Manufacturing Are Suffering. In August 2008, a married couple, both factory workers treated themselves to new cars. One month later the company laid them both off as it transferred production to Mexico. Maybe factory workers shouldn't be buying two new cars anyway. But that's not the point. This is wrong on many levels. First the jobs went overseas, which put people out of work, and economies with no way to exist due to the workers having no money to spend. Who in the government or corporate doesn't think of these things? So management makes more money due to the lower cost to produce in Mexico while the workers, assuming they get a job at all, now will most likely makes less at the new job.

At one time, there were so many manufacturing jobs that you could quit one, cross the street and easily get another. I remember the same situation in the construction industry back in the 1970s. You could get a new car every couple years and send your kids to college. Now they get student loans because the price of an education is so high, and the graduate or former student is often crippled for life with that debt. But no one is missing any meals at the high end naturally. Even if this takes another 50 years to finally destroy our country, are you sure you are OK with that?

The sad truth is that the glory days of yesteryear are gone. There are no more good decent-paying jobs, only the low end crap in the health care and fast food industry.

There are food banks distributing millions of pounds of food every year in numerous cities. People are hungry. We don't hear about people starving in the United States, but it happens. Many children eat only when they are at school, so weekends can be extremely long.

This gap plays out even at the college level. While most graduates are struggling to get a job, a few lucky ones are starting at $80,000 a year. Just more of the gap. There is something wrong when a middle-aged man or woman can't get a job for $30,000 and some snot-nosed wet-behind-the-ears, arrogant kid gets $80,000. Granted, that example is for someone on Wall Street and the older guys and gals are just as bad. I don't want to sound as though I am against the younger generation. As mentioned elsewhere, a 22 year old coming out of college has his/her difficulties finding decent work also. Not everyone has the aptitude or desire, and that should not be grounds for starvation. It again begs the question of just what advantage technology brings. Granted some technology is beneficial.

Then there are those who say this time is different due to artificially low interest rates, and hence, return on capital. This increase in wealth hasn't been due to higher growth or productivity. It's simply been a result of government interference. Again, liars figure and figures lie. Maybe a little bit of both to screw the average worker.

Supposedly the United States' manufacturing companies cannot find enough qualified workers. Next thing you know they will say that's why they sent their manufacturing overseas. In 2012 SECO Tools in Troy, Michigan, had 11 job openings, paying up to $90,000 annually. It did the right thing by paying signing bonuses and paying for retraining. Mazak Corporation in Florence, Kentucky said recently they couldn't find welders. How tough would it be to train some welders for a decent wage? They, too, are offering signing bonuses. What was so tough about that? OMAX Corporation in Kent, Washington, went one better by offering referral fees to current employees." (Rooks, 2012) Nobody questions that some jobs have become more complex. Seems like any of the above solutions would work just fine. This is one of the rare instances when a relatively cheap dollar has made it more profitable for companies to build and ship products out of the U.S. Plus, I suspect that on occasion we can still do a better job than many other countries.

No one is saying a high school dropout should receive the same pay as a smart college graduate (actually some do say that), but should it be an all or nothing game with the rich cruising on their yachts while the poor starve? Come on.

What do you think? People are standing in mission soup lines and corporate America is flush with cash... Lots of it. Duh. Wouldn't that be a hint that the system is set up wrong? Corporations are hoarding in excess of $2 trillion in cash as of 2013–14, which is 3.5 times more than in 1993. Let's see, shall we divide it up among all the shareholders and employees to make their lives easier, or shall we just keep it and pay ourselves enormous bonuses? Golly gee, Toto, what do you think the answer will be? I'm thinking a new Gulfstream, some oak paneling, and maybe a third house in the Hamptons. I repeat for effect; this has been getting worse for several decades and, even if it takes several decades, sooner or later, the poor will get fed up and somebody is going to die. I see no other solution.

Between 2001 and 2006, over 53% of national income was going to the top 1% (Stone, 2015). Even their housing is better off. While U.S. home prices did fall 33% after 2006 (Stone, 2015) —more than they did during the Great Depression—prices in Washington, D.C., San Francisco, New York, LA, and Boston, (the strongholds of the rich) are back to being just as ridiculous as before. I am reminded of the movie *Logan's Run* every time I see prices in the more sought-after areas being 10 times or more than out in the hinterland. All it takes is one person with way too much money, like Mark Zuckerberg, to overpay around $13 million for a house not worth even one tenth of that and the race is on.

Since the 1980s, over 42% of the wealth has gone to the top 1% of the population, 94% has gone to the top 20%, and the bottom 80% has split the remaining 6% (Stone, 2015).

While the rest of us are losing our shirts because of cheap labor in other parts of the world, the rich live in 40,000-square-foot mansions and throw million-dollar birthday parties.

Over one recent three-day period, 10,000 people applied for 90 jobs making washing machines in

Kentucky for $27,000 a year." (Snyder, 2010) It is extremely sad when so many people need such a small amount of money to live on, and they are unable to get even that. Nice country we have here.

The rich love third-world nations and sending our jobs to them, because they own all the factories or companies, they earn millions off of the cheap labor.

However, all you hear from the rich is a barrage of dull platitudes insinuating that they are rich because of capitalism. And then they ask, "Would you rather be living in Russia?" insinuating that communism is far worse. Well, maybe. Just to clarify, what we think of as capitalism today isn't any such thing. It's crony capitalism. Capitalism or free trade or freedom to fail just doesn't exist anymore—at least not in the good old U S of A. There is no level playing field, so any one of us could climb up by our bootstraps if we only worked hard enough. The exception may be those immigrants from third world countries who have made the decision to come, work for less, yet still save and send money back to their lesser developed country. Even though they are making more money, I'm not so sure the freedom is any better here. I also don't believe you will see any Germans, Frenchmen or Scandinavians coming here. However, the deck has been stacked against the majority of us for years—those of us not born with money. Our entire system is run on "who you know" or "who you can buy."

"Capitalists want to socialize losses after pocketing profits." Isn't that what happened with the banks after their screw ups and crimes in and around 2008? Actually not real sure whether it was criminal intent or just incompetence.

Not to be too one-sided, we should mention that, what the Russians and most others practice is not true communism either. Any time someone at the top has a lot of money, a big beautiful house and a cushy life, that's not communism. Additionally, there does seem to be a lot of killing going on in communism. Marx may have advocated some killing in order to get someone's attention, but I don't think he mentioned any killing as a normal day to day modus operandi.

The usual methodology for the CEOs amassing huge wealth for themselves is cutting jobs or cutting wage levels—meaning the workers' not themselves. CEOs can even "backdate" their stock options to when the options were worth more. When the Financial Standards Accounting Board tried to stop the practice, senators on both sides of the aisle voted it down. Gee, I wonder why? Maybe because they were in someone's back pocket?

Why didn't politicians do more in the face of the financial crisis, instead of hiding behind rhetoric like, "Too big to fail?" Because the rich can buy influence.

Lobbying may be the greatest rigging game ever devised. As of 2009, more than 30% of congressmen go on to become lobbyists. The pay is upward of $2 million a year to influence legislation (Williams, 2011). Why do banks, realtors, and insurers have hundreds of former federal employees on their payrolls as lobbyists?

According to the Ancient Greeks, humans have two sides, one called "appetite," which is the rational mind working to acquire things; the other is the "spirit," which has to do with honor, status, and religion, etc. When the spirit kicks in, and people begin to suspect things are not fair and they are being screwed, then the blood in the streets becomes a reality. This may be where the expression "Animal spirits" comes from that the Keynsians love so much.

As prevalent as Wall Street Greed is, and as nasty and evil as most in the industry are, nothing has changed over time. Wall Street has always been greedy, just like the rest of us, only with the means to do something about it. The rich getting more than their fair share is nothing new, it's been going on since the beginning of time. The only thing that might be of interest to us is that we are now very near the top of the list of greedy regimes. Only the Byzantine Empire around the year 1000 was worse with the top 1% share being around 31%. In 2013, we were at 22.5%. Others over the years were:

- China in 1880 at 21.3%
- Mexico in 1790 at 21.1%

- Rome in 14 at 16.1%
- India in 1750 at 15%
- The Kingdom of Naples in 1811 at 14.3%
- India in 1947 at 14%
- India in 1801 at 11.5%
- Brazil in 1872 at 11.2%
- England in 1801 at 8.9%
- England in 1688 at 8.7%
- Spain in 1752 at 7%

(CorpFlunky, 2014)

People—rich and poor—are mostly always greedy. There are exceptions to that rule, but very few. The rich ones don't always have a system in place that encourages debt and favors investors over working people like today. These times, they are a tryin'. The Feds and the government made it possible for the rich to get richer. This system really escalated after Nixon took us off the gold standard. And things are getting worse. It seems like we have passed the point of no return on the fulcrum. .

It's bad enough when a 70 year old can't get a job, but there are plenty of 22-year-old college graduates who can't find work either. Capitalism's trickle-down theory wouldn't be so bad if it actually worked. If even some of that money made its way to the average person, you might not mind the rich getting richer. I personally would still mind, just because of the unfairness of it all, but the problem is it isn't happening that way at all. The average person is not doing better and hasn't been for 40 years (Hamm, 2014). For emphasis, it does not matter how much taxing the rich would help; just be fair and give the rest of us a system to believe in.

We average people are so stupid or oblivious we still think Washington has our best interests at heart. But, first, the people running the show would need to have a heart; unfortunately, that does not seem to be the case. The majority of us have been putting up with lower real wages, lower standards of living, and inequality—yet we still haven't hit the streets in protest. Some American spirit.

Two Different Worlds in the United States

It definitely depends on which side of the street you walk. On the one side, the rich and powerful live large and fat (or artificially skinny), thanks to the corrupt government system and human nature. On the other side, you can find homeless and hungry people as well as those making $30–50,000 per year and struggling. This latter group, and some of the homeless as well, worked hard and studied hard. The rich will say, nothing personal; it's just business. Many of these people were let go during a downturn despite many years of loyalty and hard work. Tough. CEOs need their yachts and another Rolls. After a certain age these people may never work again because they can be replaced by some young person living at home, cheaper on insurance, and willing to work for peanuts and put in ridiculous overtime for nothing. In addition to the scrimping on the basics, the quality of life goes down as there is no money for retirement enjoyment, such as trips, spending time with elderly parents before they die, or the kids. In all likelihood these folks have to downsize from a home to an apartment. They are missing out on life and are sometimes lonely.

Want to take a look at the other side? Picture a smug, fortunate, 30-something cutie pie with a good tan, willing to sell his/her mother for a nickel, cruising on his/her yacht after a tough day screwing honest investors out of their life savings. No doubt he drives a BMW and has a McMansion. Think ski trips in the winter and beach weekends in the summer. Next you are going to tell me he deserves it. Cause he's a hard worker or something? It is more likely he inherited it, or his parents were able to send him to the best colleges, or he bamboozled his way to the top. Because he knows someone he got that job in Wall Street manipulating, stealing, cheating, and lying. Basically fraud. But on Wall Street you don't go to prison, you get bailed out because you are too big to fail, or settle out of court for a small fine.

There is a third possible player; the deadbeat. He probably does drugs, sleeps around, and fathers children all over the place, has no job, and does not pay taxes. He lives Section 8, gets welfare, free health care, and food stamps, and he doesn't pay his child support.

Yet, we don't bother to turn down the reality show on TV to consider how or why this economic inequity is happening. Like maybe through inflation, unfair advantages of the rich, and a really lousy government that is so self-serving it can't get anything done or is just bought by the rich. The number of hardworking good guys in the United States is astounding.

No wonder people are overweight and are committing suicide. More people kill themselves in the United States every year than die from car accidents or homicides (DeSilver, 2013).

The number one problem is artificial inflation and greed at the very top. This inflation was created by the Federal Reserve with the backing, cooperation, and input of the White House, Congress, and the biggest banks in the country—like JP Morgan, Goldman Sachs, Citigroup. Although the claim is they are doing all this inflating to help the middle class through the downturn (caused by them). What really happened was the rich got richer because they reduced their mortgages through cheaper money, bought a bunch more property, bought stocks at the bottom, and rode everything up. Average people with no money can't do that (Sill, 2015).

The working class got nothing except higher prices and job loss or reduction in pay and living standards. Middle-class wealth is down 45% since 2007. Thirty percent of workers in a 2013 Employee Benefit Research Institute study had less than $1,000 in savings and investments; 60% had less than $25,000. The same survey found that 76% of Americans are living paycheck to paycheck. Half of the country receives some kind of assistance from the government. Try not to get hung up on the numbers. If not exact or there are differences of opinion so be it. The basics are still there.

Some small good deeds do get rewarded, but the big rewards go to the rich and connected. Isn't that the way they planned it? Blood and Circuses? The idea originated with Romans. That's why they held the Christian/lion killings and the entertainment. They knew they had to keep the masses preoccupied. Enter the reality TV of today?

Male Peacock

If you're a male peacock, or a cardinal (the bird, not the religious one) you get the bright feathers. I guess we need to add CEOs, movie stars and sports figures to that category. Bright feathers being money. I don't even care if they are really good executives, they're grossly overpaid. What's worse, it seems quite a few are not even that good. According to Bernie Ebbers, not only don't you need to know anything about the business you are getting into, you don't have to know anything about business period.

What will get you a job as a leader in the corporate world is the same thing that will get you a woman in the mating game—outsize confidence. I don't know who is worse, the overconfident male or the idiot woman dumb enough to go for all that crap. Scientists call this "impression management." A man (or woman) with a good line of bull and a confident air gets almost anything he wants. If it's a woman, it's even more biased. A woman with good looks can write her own ticket. You gotta know where this is going, right? Any psychologist having done studies on the matter will tell you that up front, the cutie pie will get the job while the more modest person will not. Once in the position (assume a few of the modest ones slip through), the roles reverse. The overconfident, loud mouth, shoot the bull shyster will fail (unless he can keep up the charade forever, and some can). Sadly, most people will be fooled by the tall, confident, incompetent one. This bluffer is almost certainly a fool and a menace also. The modest man will, of course, usually be the better choice, being a better team player and having a much better work ethic and awareness. There are very few "Masters of the Universe."

Survival of the fittest may be somewhat overrated depending on your definition. Certainly it is a good thing to be healthy and in good shape. But that can be accomplished at 5'10" and 160 pounds getting out and playing with the kids and eating right. Along with that would come the development of your mind and heart; helping your fellow man and caring for those less fortunate. That is theoretically what we espouse. I find that inconsistent with the 6'6" ape who hits people for a living and can't spell cat. Or the basketball player. Let me assure you I am not singling out athletics. We can also discuss rock stars, movie stars, corporate execs, and reporters. Started out with the right idea but absolute power corrupts absolutely. Is there really any justification for people starving while these people get so much? Remember, if we were not allowing this to happen, it wouldn't. We buy the CDs and watch "Friends."

Would you like an example of this? Think about Andrew Fastow, the arrogant, better than everyone else, smarter than you, better looking than you, jerk at Enron. I believe he was their CFO. The penalty should have been to pull his nails out and water-board him. A mere few years, and then the book deal. What a crock. I can do this for any number of groups. Each group has its caricature—yuppie;

hillbilly white trash; loud, bully, ghetto blacks; French snobs;   German aggressiveness; British fops. See how easy this is?

Why would you pay a man $90 million to be a corporate bureaucrat? Couldn't you find others to do the work for less? Only a reckless madman would throw money around like that. The country must be full of them.

CHAPTER ONE – WHY IS GREED GOOD?

Supposedly the rich are angry at the government because of the indecision. The rest of us are too.

Die-hard religious conservatives offer up the following: Ask any Republican rich person and they will insist that the Democrat always want to tax the rich, calling them responsible, who earned their money (insinuating that it was with long hours and major personal sacrifices), to feed weed smoking, lazy, welfare recipients. Granting that there is a portion that fits that profile, it may be because the rich cream all the money off the top; and there are honest hard working people out there who are really being abused by the rich and their system. No wonder there is such animosity in our Congress. I'm not saying there isn't a grain of truth to that, just that it might have been said a bit nicer. Plus I have discussed before how many (or how few) of the rich actually did all that hard work, right?

At the decision-making level it is clear that they are inept, incompetent, and borderline criminal. I remember thirty-five years ago when banks paid 5% in savings accounts and lent on real estate at 7–7.5% and did just fine. Certainly a volatile rate environment makes it difficult—so for the money you are being paid, get to it and figure out a way. Matching deposits with lending time frames could be one way. If you created a 30–year bond then, and only then, you can make a 30–year loan. A savings deposit can only be matched with a very short-term loan (one year or so). Borrowing short term and lending long term is called dissintermediation?

Perkins and Other Jerks

If this doesn't make your blood boil, shame on you. Venture capitalist Tom Perkins compared "the progressive war on the American one percent" to Nazi Germany in the *Wall Street Journal*. Real estate magnate Sam Zell agreed, telling Bloomberg TV, "The 1% are being pummeled because it's politically convenient to do so. Zell, Wilbur Ross and John Mack have griped about the unschooled masses scapegoating America's moneyed elite." (Perkins, 2014) Persecution! Unschooled masses! Doesn't that tell you what these creeps think about the rest of us? Seriously, why doesn't some young, energetic hotshot start a revolution and selectively kill them? Just give me the chance to kill someone who calls me the unschooled masses!" Separately, Nicole Miller CEO Bud Konheim said on CNBC that Americans making $35,000 a year should stop complaining because they're much better off than people in India and China. "We've got a country that the poverty level is wealth in 99 percent of the rest of the world," he said. "So we're talking about woe is me, woe is us, woe is this." (Frank, 2014) Someone ought to kill this SOB! The French Revolution is looking pretty good. That kind of attitude is likely why Hitler and the Germans reacted in the manner they did. Besides, of the one percent, how many of them actually earned it? Probably 20% inherited it, 20% are mean spirited, and arrogant, 20% are just lucky—in the right place at the right time, 20% are "talented". So that only leaves 20%.

Letter from a Schmuck

Following is an inclusion from an article found in *Politico*, for your enjoyment and education. Hopefully you will see the same vile attitude I do. One could take this article either way. Hanauer on the side of practicality insinuates that the rich had better be careful, yet he continues to indicate that somehow the rich, including himself, are better than the rest of us .He can't seem to help himself.

Memo: From Nick Hanauer

To: My Fellow Zillionaires (See what I mean? Smart ass)

"I am one of those .01%ers, a proud and unapologetic capitalist. My friends and I own a bank. I tell you all this to demonstrate that in many ways I'm no different from you. Like you, I have been rewarded OBSCENELY for my success, with a life that the other

99.99 percent of Americans can't even imagine. Multiple homes, my own plane, etc. In 1992, I was selling pillows made by my family's business, and the Internet was a clunky novelty. But I saw pretty quickly that many of my customers, the big department store chains, were already doomed. Realizing that, seeing over the horizon a little faster than the next guy, was the strategic part of my success. Now I own a very large yacht." (Hanauer, 2014). Arrogant schmuck. Now you know just how these rich guys feel about the rest of us.

He continues, "I'm not the smartest guy you've ever met, or the hardest-working. I was a mediocre student. I'm not technical at all—I can't write a word of code. What sets me apart, I think, is a tolerance for risk and an intuition about what will happen in the future." (Hanauer, 2014*).* I'm not sure exactly how much these traits are worth. It sounds like he is just another blowhard sales type who ran rough-shod over everyone, or is just lucky.

So he admits he really can't do much of anything. Was it because he had family money? Remember the pillow story. Am I really the only one offended by every word out of this guy's mouth?

Then he goes on to warn his fellow schmucks that he sees pitchforks coming, an allusion to the Frankenstein monster movies I guess. *"At the same time that people like you and me are thriving beyond the dreams of any plutocrats in history, the rest of the country—the 99.99 percent—is lagging far behind. Inequality between the have and the have nots is at historically high levels and getting worse every day. Our country is rapidly becoming less a capitalist society and more a feudal society. Soon we will be back to late 18th-century France. Before the revolution. And so I have a message for my fellow filthy rich, for all of us who live in our gated bubble worlds: Wake up, people. It won't last. If we don't do something to fix the glaring inequities in this economy, the pitchforks are going to come for us. No society can sustain this kind of rising inequality. In fact, there is no example in human history where wealth accumulated like this and the pitchforks didn't eventually come out. You show me a highly unequal society, and I will show you a police state. Or an uprising. There are no counterexamples. None. It's not if, it's when"* (Hanauer*).*

He continues with his self-important rant, saying *"many of us think we're special because 'this is America.' We think we're immune to revolutions"* (Hanauer 2014*)*
"You're living in a dream world. What everyone wants to believe is that when things reach a tipping point and go from being merely crappy for the masses to dangerous and socially destabilizing, we're somehow going to know about that shift ahead of time. Any student of history knows that's not the way it happens.

Revolutions, like bankruptcies, come gradually, and then Bam! And then there's no time for us to get to the airport and jump on our Gulf-streams and fly to New Zealand. It's not just that we'll escape with our lives; it's that we'll most certainly get even richer" (Hanauer,) What an jerk! Anyone really think he is concerned about anyone other than himself?

Mr. delusional condemns wealthy business owners who feel they are the driving force in the economy. Many economists also believe that, so it doesn't help in finding a cure when you don't have a handle on the disease. Even though he is telling the truth on this one, I still don't like him.

Sadly, in spite of all the inequality and envy, there's no evidence of any revolution. Americans are a bunch of pansies. We follow in the footsteps of the very CEO self-confidence trait we acknowledge isn't right, only to a lesser degree. We think we can beat everyone up and are smarter than everyone else. Until someone calls our bluff. We are the best of men, we are the worst of men. Kudos to Charles Dickens. Rather than storm the gated communities, United States citizens are merely screaming at the TV. More's the pity! Seems like they are saying most of us are so stupid we don't even know what's going on and how much we are getting screwed.

Before Hanauer's pitchforks there will be other attempts at solutions. There will be higher taxes probably even though it will take time. And eventually spending cuts will be enacted. They will get attended to in the usual American way—just a second before disaster strikes. The rich will have to pay more, but they'll still be rich. The thing is, there are two problems. Yes, people want the government to raise taxes and help those less fortunate, but the people also believe the government isn't capable or trustworthy enough to do that. Tough position. That's why the Republicans can get away with consistently blocking tax hikes on the wealthy. Plus the labor unions have seen better days also, so they're no help. The other thing is, it is hard to get that consensus because the poor are almost as bad as the rich. Everyone wants something for nothing, which makes it easier for the government to twist things and stall. My editor, Jennifer, will tell you she doesn't believe this is true. She thinks two people should not have to work in a family. There is a strong opinion here that someone should stay home and care for the children, because it is a tough job and because it is better for them. I agree. She also believes people work hard and are willing to work hard. We differ there. Let's agree to disagree and say many people fall into each camp.

Even the Supreme Court can and has been bought, siding with the rich. This includes sexual harassment cases, in which the court sided with the corporations, cases in which the court sided with the drug manufacturers and 13 out of the last 16 cases (Milhiser, 2013). The elimination of limits on campaign donations favors the rich wanting to influence.

There are a few reasons for including this fellow's views. One, to show just what schmucks most of the rich are; and two, to show that even some of them know there is a problem with this inequality and it usually ends badly. You must know he's not doing this for any altruistic reasons, only to save his own skin. Due to the nasty, arrogant bent to his conversation, and an undertone of contempt for others, he is hard to stomach even though he may be right. To beat a dead horse again, was he just lucky? Said he was working in the family business so he didn't start from scratch. Although the percentages are sheer bluff on my part, I stand behind my breakdown of the rich. A certain percentage inherited, another percentage just got lucky—right place, right time—a third group really are cutthroat and will win at any costs so they do have a leg up on easier-going people. That only leaves a small portion of truly hardworking, smart, and decent human beings who are rich.

Technology

How is it possible that the world's richest and most technologically advanced economy ever, operating during a 50-year period that included the invention of the Internet ... the triumph of capitalism in China and Russia ... and a landing on the moon—the most productive half-century in human history—failed so miserably to help mankind be happier, improve working conditions, and increase job security?

Have we really improved? Automatic transmissions are now electric, but are they any better? And what about the expense? Sometimes simple is better, not always, but sometimes. What makes it better? It would seem that it should last longer and run smoother. It would really be nice if it were easier and less expensive to repair. That is not the case.

How about the leisure time bonus? Actually we work harder for less money now. It takes two people in a family now to do the same as one used to and perhaps because of that the divorce rate is up.

Will technology destroy American society? The one side says that throughout history technology has replaced the jobs that it eliminated with new and better jobs. I wonder. Sure, I like air conditioning, refrigeration, indoor plumbing, electricity, a basic telephone, antibiotics, and the ability to get around better and faster. (Most people today don't know what an outhouse is.) And for many decades things did improve. Granted radio and TV are really neat (totally abused), but communication is important. Good technology does not appear to be the case for the last few decades. It feels sometimes as though technology is directed toward gadgetry. At least for the middle class in the first world societies. That's assuming there is any middle class left. At this point those in the third world developing countries are still improving their lifestyles. That may be because most of them were living in huts without clean drinking water. Easy to improve on that.

The money saved by technology was supposed to go to those workers either made redundant for training or to those left behind who were supposed to have an easier time of it. In reality, the money went to the top brass. That is not the only reason although it is probably enough of one that if corrected things would get back on track. That means the average person could sleep at night without fear of his/her family starving to death.

Pundits make light of this "rise of the machines" like it's still a movie. Certainly there is an issue with being replaced by machines. At least until we improve as a planet more in line with what Ray Bradbury and Gene Roddenberry intimated.

A few danger signs for the immediate future: Kiosks to take your order at McDonald's; hamburger making machines; robotic bartenders. How important is it really, to have a new app on your iPhone? Amazon and Netflix do not really help our standard of living or comfort, they only help us buy and watch more garbage. GPS seems like a good thing. More games to play and waste time with, hmmm--not so much.

I suspect the higher minimum wage issue, whether you favor it or not, has nothing to do with technology replacing workers. Although high wages and benefits might induce management to look toward machines, management would go for the machines regardless of what wages were paid. Also, when naysayers ask why business owners shouldn't replace workers with machines", the answer is sooner or later the workers will rise up and kill you because they have no incentive to do anything else. When you get up in the morning in Venezuela in the barrio with a hut with no windows and a mud floor and no job prospects, why not resort to a life of crime—all they can do is kill you, and your family is dying of malnutrition anyway.

It's the low-wage unskilled workers who get replaced by automated systems. Any doubt about that?

More efficient scheduling means more workers on duty during peak sales times without being overstaffed during lulls. Good for business—bad for workers since the prices for goods and services they have to still pay are going up.

What have we improved? Automobile transmissions are now electric—how are they better? Less expensive? No. Last longer? No. More expensive to repair? Yes. Work better? How? Do we have more leisure? No, we work harder; two people in a family now work, the divorce rate is up. We seem to be going the wrong way regarding the poor and their standards. We need to cut out overtime and give to others—makes for no family life anyway for those who have to do the work.

Job growth is stagnant and even those people who do have a job are not in a position to spend because their incomes are not growing. That goes a long way to explain why consumption growth has been so weak.

On the poor end of the job spectrum the bulk of spending goes to pay for non-durable items—such as gas, food, and clothing—all of which always seem to only go up, never down. If there is any money left that is what gets spent on cars, appliances, and furniture. Not so with the rich.

None of this takes away from the fact that we in the United States have a lousy secondary school system and are churning out a criminal element without basic life and work skills, except for a select few. What little education young people do get is channeled in the wrong direction. We are turning out a lot of history majors, liberal arts majors, and sociologists. And college, like health insurance, here in the United States, is outrageously expensive. Would it be nice if everyone had the opportunity to attend college? Sure. Would they want to or are they qualified to? Not so sure.

Will there be problems with that. Yep. As some of those "college material" individuals enter the trades environment they will push out others who are not as smart. It's a problem yes, but maybe a step forward at least. Then there is the supposition that technology isn't able to replace those jobs such as plumbing, electricity, welding, construction, and automotive mechanics. My guess is if they can make hamburgers they can weld.

The benefits of technology have not made life easier for workers as was promised, merely reduced the number of jobs available without a plan for other work or more affordable leisure.

The point is, who cares if the average worker makes a difference or not? Concede for a moment the argument that the CEO is all that matters. First, let's all quit and see how well he does without workers. No? OK, then go at it from a more macro humanitarian level. Yes, human nature is lousy, but are we not trying to improve it all the time? Isn't that what civilization is all about?

Technology has played a *major* role in the relentless redistribution of wealth. The Internet helps the rich and connected reach more people and earn more money. Plus the supercomputers run fast and sophisticated algorithms keep the rich ahead of the Mom and Pops. During the first quarter of 2010, four of the biggest banks in the United States—Goldman Sachs, JP Morgan Chase, Bank of America and Citigroup—had a 'perfect quarter,' with zero days of trading losses (Doyle, 2010). How is it possible to be perfect? Until recently, the big banks traded derivatives (an instrument like a bond that's value depends on the underlying asset it came from or is a part of) between themselves, with absolutely no oversight, making fortunes. "The derivatives market is equivalent to 41 times the United States' GDP." (Williams, 2011) Remember, mortgage-backed securities? Just a small part of the total derivatives market.

Have you caught your breath? Think the rich are being unfairly judged? Think again. Computer trading programs on Wall Street are just one of the latest vehicles for the rich to get a jump on the rest of us. This is sheer criminal activity. Don't get me wrong. The rich are not perfect, and the computers every once in a while make a mistake. They seem to have trouble computing the level of panic in the market and sometimes interest rate fluctuations. Supposedly that's what happened with Long-Term Capital Management back in the late 1990s.

When interest rates swerved, the computer didn't anticipate it. Incidentally, that was a "mere" $4.6 billion problem, and it caused market turmoil for several months. I wonder what might happen if a $400 trillion derivatives market blows up? I'm sure the "Boys from Brazil" in Wall Street will find a way to make the average person pay for it.

Most of this and other theories usually depend on which side of the fence you are on. As a refresher, the two sides break down as follows: Milton Friedman, for the capitalists, says, "There is one and only one social responsibility of business--to use its resources and engage in activities designed to increase its profits so long as it stays within the rules of the game, which is to say, engages in open and free competition without deception or fraud.'

The more socially conscious argument is summed up by John Mackey, the CEO of Whole Foods, who said,
'I believe that the enlightened corporation should try to create value for all of its constituencies. From an investor's perspective, the purpose of the business is to maximize profits. But that's not the purpose for other stakeholders--for customers, employees, suppliers, and the community. Each of those groups will define the purpose of the business in terms of its own needs and desires, and each perspective is valid and legitimate.'"
(Jones, 2013). Profit is good, but only as a means to an

end. So, eat drink and be merry; or health, happiness, safety, security and leisure. Sounds OK to me.

Downloading a high-definition movie takes about seven seconds in Seoul, Hong Kong, Tokyo, Zurich, Bucharest and Paris, and people pay as little as $30 a month for that connection. In Los Angeles, New York and Washington, downloading the same movie takes 1.4 minutes for people with the fastest Internet available, and they pay $300 a month for the privilege, according to the New America Foundation's Open Technology Institute. The reason for this isn't a lack of technology, it's a lack of competition. We have monopolies here. Monopolies are fertile grounds for high CEO pay and bonuses.

CHAPTER TWO - HISTORY

Another Republican idea I just don't get is how much we all benefit from the rich getting richer. If that were true, then how come the wealth gap is over 300? If so, why not just get it over with and give one guy all the money. Just think how rich we'd all be then!

Concentration of wealth hurts the little guy and the average guy. That's because what goes into their pockets comes out of ours. The less obvious but equally important thing is, it has not proven to be a boom to society either. Just because you have an iPhone doesn't mean you are better off than those slaves building pyramids back in Egypt. How much longer do you think we have? Right now we are in the worst inequity position since the height of the Byzantine Empire in the year 1000, when the top one percent had 31% of the wealth. As of 2013 our top one percent has 22.5%. (CorpFlunky, 2014)

Although current times are as bad as it gets, bullying has been around a long time. All the wrong values are rewarded, but it's nothing new. The Roman Empire existed on tribute obtained by brute force two thousand years ago (Lachman, 2014).

Captains of Industry

In spite of how bad we are now, we do have great examples of unfairness in the past. The men who made the United States—the captains of industry of the late 1800s and early 1900s—were ruthless, greedy SOBs. They had to be the best in their own minds. Even Carnegie (and he was one of the better ones) stuck his head in the sand while Frick (his second in command) killed people in his name at the Homestead Steel Plant strike in 1892. Not only was he responsible for Homestead, but also he was a member of the club that caused the Johnstown Flood in 1888. One of the biggest of the "Captains", or "Robber Barons", whichever you prefer, John D. Rockefeller, just wasn't a very nice man. Another of those mean people claiming to be deeply religious. Winning at all and any cost. That's the American mantra. All you had to do was look at J.P. Morgan to tell he was a schmuck—steely-eyed cutthroat. How is that good? From an inequality standpoint, JP Morgan was as conspicuous a consumer as there ever was. You could stop with his yacht the Corsair and his home at 219 Fifth Ave and make your point.

Very few knowledgeable people have anything good to say about J.P. Morgan. It seems a consensus that he was not a nice man. No question he had the confidence (along with inherited money), was brash, a brute, a barbarian, intimidating, used force, used corrupt trickery and used strangleholds. It was profit at any cost. And profit and power there was. Morgan was responsible for the formation of General electric, which did get rid of soot and death by gas fumes, US Steel, which build ships (for commerce), Railroads, which did help to open up new territory for living and exploration of natural resources and the Panama Canal which shortened shipping time and saved money, for the rich I'm betting. But wouldn't all of that occur anyway regardless of who owned the entities? What was the trickle down percentage for the average person? Meanwhile working hours increased and workplace fatalities increase. Morgan also participated heavily in the formation, (through raising money usually) of AT & T, International Harvester, Case, Atlas Portland Cement and many others.

He was another Donald Trump type, having inherited Daddy's money for a big leg up to start. Morgan did fail several times but that only proves it's hard to lose all the money Daddy left you if you have infinite chances. "While some multimillionaires robber barons started in poverty, most did not. A study of the origins of 303 textile, railroad and steel executives of the 1870s showed that 90% came from middle or upper class families." (Zinn, 1980) How did he do it? Putting companies together, bailing out companies- all of which takes a group of investors. The process of creating a monopoly through the elimination of competition and the maximization of profits by slashing the workforce and reducing their wages is named after JP Morgan. It was called Morganization.

Morgan was another of the typical rich who escaped military service during the Civil War by paying $300 to a substitute to fight for him. During the war he buys five thousand rifles at $3.50 each and sells them on at $22 apiece. The rifles are defective and some shoot off the thumbs of the soldiers firing them. Don't see much of that in the history books.

In Morgan's battle with George Westinghouse, Morgan used his enormous wealth to force Westinghouse to sign over Tesla's patents. Money talks. At the same time he pushed Edison out of the company. Not a nice man. Morgan and his cronies were so powerful their money bought the election of 1896 simply by outspending their opponent by 5 to 1. Plus voting was a more public affair and workers know they may be fired if seen to be voting for the opponent. If you think no harm is done by such men, sadly recall that the man who shot President McKinley was a factory worker who lost his job in a JP Morgan takeover.

Interestingly, Morgan controlled the White Star Shipping Line, owner of the Titanic. He was supposed to be on that infamous voyage. Some people might view that as proof that there really is no justice.

Even Edison thwarted Nikola Tesla regarding alternating current. He refused to look at, consider, or help with it while Tesla was working for him and heavily advertised with propaganda in an attempt to discredit the process later. It is said that Edison reneged on his agreement to pay Tesla for his work and discoveries." (King, 2013)

McClosky and Creative Destruction

Economic historian Deirdre McCloskey doesn't see the Industrial Revolution and beyond happening on the backs of slaves, but by "Changes in the way people thought, and especially how they thought about each other." I'd say there was a better chance for the slave argument, even if not entirely correct. (McClosky, 2006)

McCloskey insinuated that people started to like "creative destruction." (McClosky, 2006) What a load. The average person not only doesn't have a clue what the phrase means but also certainly does not like any kind of change, especially if that "creative destruction" loses them their job. Setting that aside, she goes on to say, "Creativity destroys old stuff and old ways of doing things, and when people started to like it, wealth and prosperity began to happen for the masses." Not only not true but not even provable.

In the old days people who merely bought and sold things for a living were scorned as "cheaters." Apparently there is less shame in that now. McCloskey reminds us that in 1800 the average daily wage was $3 in today's money (McClosky, 2006). But what did the average item cost? In addition to not comparing apples to apples, the entire manner of living was different, both good and bad. The issue to add in here is the necessity of some of the technological improvement in our life. Think iPhone/iPad.

She somehow believes the middle class was given dignity and liberty for the first time in human history, and because of that, suddenly the masses became literate, automation took hold, innovation broke out everywhere, civil rights took hold, and leisure time, information, and advances in all areas kept piling up (McClosky, 2010). All because of dignity and liberty? You've got to be kidding me.

CHAPTER THREE - WHO ARE THESE GUYS?

Here's a list of requirements if you want to qualify for the position of Chief Executive Officer (CEO): invest less in legal compliance and violate the law, pay kickbacks to secure business, under-report profits to avoid taxes, be willing to fire workers who have been with the company for decades, accept a lion's share of any profits for yourself- and if there isn't any profit, take some anyway, and manipulate, manipulate, manipulate. (Stucke, 2013) Qualified? Well, come on down!

Greedy Owners

Why are average U.S. consumers still strapped? Simple. Companies in the United States and their owners are gorging themselves at the trough more today than ever in the history of the world. And that's saying something considering those robber barons and the captains of industry in the late 1800s referred to before.

In case you have been with Rip Van Winkle for the last five years, U.S. corporations have made obscene profits. Plus by cutting costs (firing people), share prices have gone up due to your idiot government providing free money and the firms buying back stock. Thanks to their greed, unemployment (or underemployment) is still a problem. And if you are lucky enough to have a job, your wages are mired in the 1970s as to purchasing power. Wage growth is the slowest in 70 years (Whitney, 2015). America's corporations and their owners have never had it better.

People don't get it! If corporations and shareholders are doing so well, why is the economy so poor? Because all of the money has gone to the top. The stock market is going up but that is not a good reflection of the main street economy, and yes, corporations are making a bundle but most of the profits have been skimmed off for the upper management. The corporations are money making machines thanks to cheap government money to borrow and international markets, but the profit just isn't trickling down to the workers. The less the corporations pay in wages—less than ever as a share of gross domestic product (GDP)—the less consumers have to spend. And the less consumers have to spend, the slower the economy grows because consumer spending is revenue for other companies. So, not only is the average person struggling now but also this greed will eventually bring the entire economy to a standstill. Short-term profits at the expense of long-term value creation. If you spend your money paying CEOs or making quarterly profits look good there is no money left to invest in plant and production for later. You can't have your cake and eat it too. Second rate country already.

Why is it that people believe capitalism says companies have to pay their employees as little as possible? Granted, it usually seems like a zero sum game in which if one side wins, another has to lose because there is only so big a pot, so take from the workers and get more for yourself, but as outlined above, sooner or later the chickens come home to roost. There's also no law of capitalism that says companies have to maximize short term profits. That's just a load of crap that owners of United States' companies made up to justify grabbing as much of the company's profits as possible for themselves and Wall Street made up to make more fees (churning).

Don't get swayed by the argument that economic weakness is the fault of too much regulation and too many taxes. That's partially true, of course, but takes a backseat to greed. Even regulation and taxes fall dis-proportionally on smaller companies. The big guys have plenty of lawyers, you know.

Would you like to have an example of just who has all the money and runs the country—could he be a typical CEO? This is the kind of person who gets ahead. The information is from October 2012.

David Siegel and his wife, Jackie, built the largest house in the United States, known as "Versailles." They became symbols of obscene spending, debt, and real estate in the United States. He's an ostentatious, nasty, greedy schmuck.

The Siegel overreaching company (Westgate Resorts) got in trouble due to too much debt during the crisis and the Siegels' home went into foreclosure. How did he get out of foreclosure and how much of a haircut did the banks take? According to Siegel, they cut back on the use of their jet, took the kids out of private school, and gave up some of their staff. Poor babies.

This guy defines excess and debt, and he's giving advice? Why? Because he is a two-faced, greedy, selfish, mean, sleazebag, hypocrite who likes to hear himself talk. Even his wife is involved in a reality TV show. Reality TV says it all.

According to Siegel, "People like me who made all the right decisions and invested in themselves are being forced to bail out all the people who didn't. The people that overspent their paychecks suddenly feel entitled to the same luxuries that I earned and sacrificed 42 years of my life for " (Berfield, 2012) I'll bet he has screwed everyone he ever dealt with, and was also lucky or inherited some of the money.

Siegel said he's not acting out of self-interest but for the interest of his workers. Yet, while Westgate has never been more profitable, the company has 5,000 fewer workers than in 2007 (Berfield, 2012).

He continued by saying, just prior to the elections in November 2012, "if Obama is reelected and imposes Obamacare and higher taxes, if any new taxes are levied on me or my company, Rather than grow this company I will be forced to cut back. This means fewer jobs, less benefits, and certainly less opportunity for everyone" (Berfield, 2012) He said he might even shut down the company. If that's not a threat, I don't know what is!

Siegel stressed that he wasn't out to intimidate his workers into voting for Romney. "I can't tell anyone to vote," he said. "I want my employees to be educated on what could happen to their future if the wrong person is elected" (Berfield, 2012)
What a jerk! I'd spend my last dollar trying to bring this guy down.

Psychopaths

Psychopaths are the 1% of the general population that aren't burdened by conscience. Psychopaths have a profound lack of empathy. They use other people callously and remorselessly for their own ends. They seduce victims with a hypnotic charm that masks their true nature as pathological liars, master con artists, and heartless manipulators. Easily bored, they crave constant stimulation, so they seek thrills from real-life "games" they can win — and take pleasure from their power over other people." They don't care that you have thoughts and feelings. They have no sense of guilt or remorse." They are unethical schemers. These psychos make a practice of inflicting pain and suffering on thousands of people who had lost their jobs, or their life's savings. Some of those victims would succumb to heart attacks or commit suicide. (Deutschman, 2005)

Psychopaths ruthlessly seek their own selfish interests — "shareholder value" — without regard for the harms they cause to others.

For corporate psychopaths especially you can add selfish, have no sense of guilt, are glib with superficial charm, have a grandiose sense of self-worth, are pathological liars, are shallow (very cold, yet can show dramatic emotional displays that are actually playacting); lack empathy; and fail to accept responsibility. In many cases, that very type is hired deliberately because the investors/board wants a jerk to decimate the company. No company wants an honest salesman. So we are our own worst enemy.

The job recruiters should place somewhere in their search ads, the phrase "must have an MBA but lack a conscience."

"I always said that if I wasn't studying psychopaths in prison, I'd do it at the stock exchange," (Deutschman, 2005) Well put, Mr Deutschman.

Wars and corporations seem to be fertile ground for psychopaths.

The second group- the violent unsuccessful psychos- are the criminals behind bars. They are chronically unstable, antisocial, and socially deviant. Funny thing is, at least you know they are the bad guys.

Psychopaths are typically very likable. They make us believe that they reciprocate our loyalty and friendship. It goes against our intuition that a small percentage of people can be so different from the rest of us — and so evil. Good people don't want to believe it." (Stout, 2005)

Some say there is a subgroup buried in psychopathy called narcissism. These are merely insensitive egotists out for improving humanity somehow, although poor listeners and touchy about criticism. (Maccoby, 2003) Maccoby suggests that Apple's Steve Jobs, General Electric's Jack Welch, Microsoft's Bill Gates, and Southwest Airlines' Herb Kelleher as "productive narcissists. (Maccoby) Nothing ever written about Steve Jobs would elevate him anywhere near that definition. Granted, generally they do have a vision of improving the world, even if to their specifications. This personality trait can be useful if matched with a control minded manager. (Maccoby)

Europe is far ahead of the United States in trying to deal with psychological abuse and manipulation at work. The "anti-bullying" movement in Europe has produced new laws in France and Sweden. Harvard's Stout suggests that the relentlessly individualistic culture of the United States contributes a lot to our problems. She points out that psychopathy has a dramatically lower incidence in certain Asian cultures, where the heritage has emphasized community bonds rather than glorified self-interest. "If we continue to go this way in our Western culture," she says, "evolutionarily speaking, it doesn't end well." (Stout, 2005)

Knowing your enemy does have its merits. The psychopaths in prison are easy to spot. You know when you meet one there is danger. The psychopaths on Wall Street and in the office of the CEO are a bit harder to recognize. That goes for commercial bankers, too. Because they wear pinstriped suits you believe they are either your friend or harmless. So you let your guard down and get hurt. It's like talking to a friend who says, "I can't understand why he did that." Of course you can't, you're not a psychopath. You don't lack empathy, you are not amoral, without feelings for other people. Man, that's scary.

Have you had a call lately from some cold calling stockbroker? The guy would cut out your liver for a nickel. He's just a vulture in training. He will get worse as he moves up the ladder. The havoc these sleazebags cause include lost jobs (for others), lost life savings, and sometimes even broken families or suicides. These people can destroy lives. However, just like a hero in war time, these heartless human beings can achieve huge corporate triumphs.

"A few years ago the Canadian Press reported on a talk Robert Hare gave on psychopathy to about 150 police officers. He began his talk with pictures of Mafia hit men and sex offenders. But then the pictures were replaced with pictures of top executives from WorldCom, which had just declared bankruptcy, and Enron, which imploded only months earlier. 'These are cold-blooded individuals,' Hare said. 'They don't care that you have thoughts and feelings. They have no sense of guilt or remorse.' He ended by saying that if he were not studying psychopaths in prison, he'd do it on Wall Street." (Fry, Pinstriped Psychopaths, 2005)

Professor Hare wants to screen potential CEOs for psychopathic traits. Why not? We screen police officers and teachers. (Deutschman, 2005) We give drug test to virtually everyone, especially at the lower end of the job market. Would you rather have a druggie do nothing, be disruptive and steal small amounts from you or a CEO who would potentially ruin your life by costing you your job and every cent you have?

According to Professor Hare, psychopaths are broken down into two sections, the merely ruthless and the violent. Or the successful and the unsuccessful. (Deutschman, 2005) The CEOs and criminals.

I don't know of any study on the subject, but it seems as though there is a direct proportion between the heartache they cause and the riches they obtain for themselves.

"Robert J. Samuelson, taking the opposite view, wrote that these brutal corporate executives can produce a greater good. The obsessive drive to improve profits, though cold-blooded, also creates often-overlooked social benefits," he asserts. Advancing productivity—a fancy term for efficiency and a byproduct of the quest for profits—is the wellspring of higher living standards." (Fry, Pinstriped Psychopaths, 2005) What clap trap! It is immaterial whether true or not, the end does not justify the mean. Not only that, but there is no recent evidence that that's true. It's a social evil and a lousy evolutionary stride.

People like Samuelson are somehow attempting to canonize villains, "make it so, Joe," by putting lipstick on a pig. You lost me with the use of words like brutal, obsessive, and cold-blooded. I would think long and hard about using the word charismatic in any good way also. We never really got to self-serving lunatic. The Daily Reckoning, a financial newsletter, had a great and poignant line. They said, "There is a very fine line between creative destruction and creative annihilation." (Fry, Pinstriped Psychopaths, 2005) Great line!

I could go on all day with examples of bad guys, however, names you should probably store away for your next beer night would include: Enron's Andrew Fastow, Sunbeam's "The Chainsaw" Al Dunlap, and Worldcom's Bernie Ebbers. Ebbers was the guy who made famous the defense that he was just an old dumb guy who didn't know what was going on. This from a highly paid CEO. Dunlop- "What do you say about a guy who didn't attend his own parents' funerals? He allegedly threatened his first wife with guns and knives. She charged that he left her with no food and no access to their money while he was away for days." (Deutschman, 2005) We should screen these people (congratulations ladies, you have made the cut, thanks to the likes of Carly Fiorina) or simply line them up and shoot them. I prefer the latter although it has been pointed out to me that there will always be others to take their place, therefore, some kind of system overhaul is more in order.

A few more examples of our boys in action follow: Manipulative? Louis B. Mayer was said to be a better actor than any of the stars he employed at MGM, able to turn on the tears at will to evoke sympathy during salary negotiations with his actors. Callous? Henry Ford hired thugs to crush union organizers, deployed machine guns at his plants, and stockpiled tear gas. He cheated on his wife with his teenage personal assistant and then had the younger woman marry his chauffeur as a cover. Lacking empathy? Hotel magnate Leona Helmsley shouted profanities at and summarily fired hundreds of employees allegedly for trivialities, like a maid missing a piece of lint. Remorseless? Soon after Martin

Davis ascended to the top position at Gulf & Western, a visitor asked why half the offices were empty on the top floor of the company's Manhattan skyscraper. "Those were my enemies," Davis said. "I got rid of them." Deceitful? Oil baron Armand Hammer laundered money to pay for Soviet espionage. Grandiosity? Sounds like Donald Trump. (Deutschman, 2005)

      The advocates for sleazebags would say these people are merely being tough. Hard to say, but it seems like you had better learn the difference. Right after you stop loving these guys for higher profits and share prices. Assuming they had anything to do with it in the first place. We all seem to not care about mass job layoffs as long as it's someone else; you know, at a distance.

      "As a nation we are willing to overlook the fact that CEOs are callous, conning, manipulative, deceitful, verbally and psychologically abusive, remorseless, exploitative, self-delusional, irresponsible, and are megalomaniacs" (Deutschman, 2005). You get what you pay for. We worship top executives who seem charismatic, visionary, and tough. As long as they appear to be making us money, we're willing to overlook that they can also be all of the above bad traits and sadly insensitive to hurting others.

Psychopathy is destructive, no matter whether it roams the back streets or Wall Street.

If allowed, this gap in wages will continue to increase until the system can't take it—Newton's Law of motion. It is already happening—we are just taking the money from the lower classes.

Do you really think CEOs work harder? Not really. Besides, I don't care. Reasonableness is the key word here. We'll deal with the derelicts at the bottom on welfare later. Right now we need to establish why one human being is worth 500 times the average. I know lots of people who get up at 5:30 AM and do hard physical work all day. Is there more stress in the corporate offices? Only for a few if they care—most don't. Stress is stress if it is your last dollar or puts food on your table. This doesn't even begin to address the fact that the CEO will have salted away a bundle for a rainy day. If not, shame on them. So there is no downside for them at all. We need to remember that in general, no one person can be singularly responsible for success. And if so, then they are singularly responsible for the loss. Therefore, as a bare minimum, CEOs should not get a bonus when the company loses money. In fact, they should take a pay cut when times are bad. Top executives need to share in the bloodletting. And it can't just be proportional. If you take 90% of my pay as an average worker, I am left to starve. If you take 90% from a CEO, they only have a million left to struggle by with. Tsk, tsk. Time for another French Revolution.

Greed Verses Enterprise

So where do you draw the line between greed and enterprise? And oftentimes, doesn't it start out as enterprise and evolve into greed? Knowing the difference between greed and enterprise isn't easy. If the reward is reasonable for hard work, and if you contribute to the wealth and opportunities for others, employment, better incomes, and living standards of others we would have to lean a bit toward enterprise.

The right thinks greed is vital to the functioning of our economy. In the essay, "The Virtue of Greed," economist Walter Williams wrote, "it's greed and not compassion that gets things done (Williams, 2011)." What an ass! Seriously? Is that really what centuries of history has evolved into, and how you want society to be during your lifetime? Also, since when is greed or making money a virtue or life in and of itself?

The left asks, "When is enough, enough?"

Who do you think is correct? Of course, if you are a business owner, nothing I say will convince you.

There is a good chance that this lack of moral clarity is threatening to destroy us. It certainly has brought governing to a standstill in our government.

Since the beginning of time a few at the top (the aristocracy) lived high on the hog by taking from the poor. Thomas Aquinas said, "One man cannot over-abound in external riches without another man lacking them." (Aquinas, 1265) So the Zero Sum Game has been around for a long time. I find it amusing that those on the right, the conservative Republicans, who are thought to be more religious, have the most trouble with this religious proposition- the Sin of Greed.

There is little argument that one of the problems we have is the huge sums being paid at the top. Never let it be said that some people are not worth more than others. There are some real losers out there. But some of those losers are already at the top due to Daddy's money. Not all successful people got where they are due to any righteous moves. Granting the contributions by Microsoft's Bill Gates, just how much should he have made? At least Bill and Melinda Gates are giving back in huge ways. In the case of the other computer gurus—same question. Not to take anything away from Mark Zuckerberg's accomplishments and brainpower, but, is he really worth thousands (or millions) of times the money of an engineer at IBM? And, what is he doing to help the world besides cyber bullying and making people feel depressed about their lives? It has become way too easy to use the Internet to leverage yourself into millions.

In the case of sport's figures—do they really add anything of value to society? Escapism maybe? Another way to waste hard-earned money instead of saving. But only the rich can make it to the big events. We just saw Tom Brady flaunting his wealth by attending two big sports events in one day: The Kentucky Derby and the big fight. How many families could that money have helped?

Some athletes use performance-enhancing drugs—great role models and contributions, right?

As documented earlier, Accountants find ways to overstate short-term earnings to increase earnings and bonuses because most of the financial system operates on a quarterly earnings basis and bonuses are based on that time period. Companies use political connections to cripple their competitors. Even the conscience challenged admit that politicians are, for the most part, greedy. For the money through corruption, for the power to impose their will and get more money, through corporate bailouts, subsidies, and providing protection from competitors; they're generally a poor lot. Yet they get rich!

I agree that thinking all wealthy people are greedy is not exactly reasonable. Pretty close, though. Likewise, to suggest that to strive for a better life is the same as greed isn't fair either. That's shortsighted and also stifles a lot of our rights and incentives. A desire to work hard and succeed shouldn't be wrong in and of itself. It depends on how you go about it. And, yes, there are a preponderance of schmucks at the top. It does appear, however, necessary to be a pushy, deceitful human being to get ahead. A little too general?

Military Corporations

Just pause for thought. Any time someone says they run their company like the military, run for the door. I could give you several examples of wonderful people in the military, from the great Major who took me under his wing; the savvy old Sergeant Major who diplomatically brought me in line; the S3 Sergeant First Class, who was married, had a regular life, and only wanted to help others and mind his own business. All exceptions. The business of the military is to kill people and to do that you must train individuals to follow blindly and create wars to go fight. All in all a very nasty setup. And people die! Yet that is usually the mindset of the CEO in major corporations and in fact, many hire from the military pool for that reason. Same aggressive attitude.

Speaking of the military, that group of CEOs catering to the military is doing quite nicely, thank you. "In the first four years after 9/11, the CEOs of the top 34 defense companies made a total of $984 million (an average of $7.7 million a year each even then)." (Bonner, Excessive CEO Salaries Based on Confidence Rather Than Performance, 2007b)

Notwithstanding, they are schmucks in a "profession" that destroys lives and costs a fortune; would they be 44 times more responsible than a general with 20 years of experience (bear in mind I don't like the generals any better), or 308 times more than an enlisted soldier (paid $25,085) or 19 times more than even the President himself?

The best way to describe the art of making war, and I use the word art very facetiously (because there is no art relating to the making of war), is to call it a complete sham. Especially those fought today. It seems painfully clear to one so average that we are being taken to the cleaners. There is generally no reason to enter into the conflict, and once we are there, we never use the strength we have to win; we just play at it to spend money and keep the military industrial complex in bonbons. Bottom line as it relates to this book: Its money and a lot of it, going to the wrong people for the wrong reason.

Ayn Rand

We are talking here about Inequality. How does Ayn Rand play into that? Because she, through her books, contributed to the current day notion that individualism is somehow to be sought. She leaves little room for sympathy for others. Let the chips fall where they may and those who can't keep up can, and should, fall by the wayside. In her philosophy there is no room for compassion and empathy, and certainly no place for collective action of any kind. That sounds pretty much like the attitude most of those at the top have today. Nothing is important except the almighty dollar.

It justifies and extols human greed and egotism, the very essence of this book. Somehow this has had a profound effect on many influential people. That's a little scary.

Like so many of us- probably most of us- she is subjective and dismissive of things she feels no need for, or disagrees with. Objectivism (her philosophy) seems to have no tolerance for opposing views. It's pretty adamant and there is no room for questioning. Like religious fanaticism. Extreme views are usually defensive against criticism. The philosophy is over simplified. Right or wrong. With me or against me. It doesn't seem to allow for catastrophe or bad luck. I don't know about you but if my child gets cancer, all bets are off. I'd kill anyone who got in my way. My integrity and my sense of fair play is out the window.

Can you imagine the United States without the collective effort that provided the Social Security blanket? What about making sure everyone is healthy and has a good education? No matter how nice things are in some valley in Colorado for John Galt, physical security is still an issue as long as human nature demands violence to take something from others.

Ayn Rand is a lot easier to take when you're twenty than when you're sixty.

Rand says private enterprise would take care of roads, schools, hospitals etc. History says otherwise. Private enterprise, until the greed factor is addressed and corrected, will go where there is a profit to be made, which means not into poor neighborhoods. As for the private army thing she suggests, again, are you kidding? Look how well that works in Africa where these bullies rape, pillage, kidnap and murder. Why is it that the "Ruby Ridge" survivalist operates on the philosophy, "he who has the most guns wins?" That may have been OK when there was a Saber-Toothed Tiger outside waiting to eat us, but it ain't the Stone Age anymore.

She is against the tax system. I'm not crazy about our tax system either, but tie this into the private enterprise discussion and ask yourself where the money will come from to get things done? Is our system fair? No. So fix the system.

On the positive side, it may train or teach you to evaluate critically and impartially. And there is little doubt that she hit the nail on the head when it comes to worthless, lazy, pig-headed, unreasonable government officials. No doubt the welfare system is broken and leaking out deadbeats. A criminal situation second only to overpaid business management and talent. Rand's Objectivism is worth reading to make us think. It points to what might be. Just remember to pick and choose. Things like do what you love and be happy. It does point out some pretty crummy people in our society. Remember though to come away asking, is there any virtue in rational selfishness?

Talent

Talent is a lot more difficult to criticize than Corporate CEO pay. Ask yourself why? As much as we beat up on a CEO making $50,000,000 a year, here's a guy or gal who usually has a substantial education, is at least fairly cleaver and has a good work ethic. We've also discussed the probability that they are psychopaths but that is beside the point. Compare that to a football player who dropped out of high school or college (or was simply passed because he played sports), belches at the table, beats up his wife, abuses dogs, and is generally an all-around poor role model. He also makes $50,000,000. So how come? This dilemma seems to fall back on the public even more. It's that human factor that wants to idolize someone, plus I guess, would rather watch a game on TV than help with the housework or mow the lawn.

Those that disagree say that athletes deserve every penny they make. It takes longer to train an athlete than to train people in other jobs (Doubtful-besides, what your point?) Jock supporters continue with, athletes make many sacrifices for the work they do. Yeah, I see them at the clubs until all hours, working so hard. Sunday afternoon addicts say athletes risk being injured, and they must be away from their home for long periods. So, what about truck drivers and construction workers? The final idiotic statement is that their careers don't usually last as long time as other people's, they can only earn big salaries for a very short time and many of them retire at the age of thirty. Awwwwwww! Poor babies. Another rationale is, if athletes don't get the money, it'll only go into club owner's pocket. Between ticket sales, merchandise, television deals, concessions, owners get rich. It's only fair that the players get some of it. Fair? Since when did fair enter into anything? Besides, again, two wrongs don't make a right. It is said that they earn no more than rock or movie stars. Again, lump them all in that boiling cauldron. Remember in the third grade, "Well, Johnny did it".

How about the excuse that they are stronger, faster, and more talented? So is a wild animal but I don't want to pay them obscene amounts of money. It is also said that they are role models. No wonder we're in trouble. Are the tickets more expensive because the salaries are high or are the salaries high because the tickets are more expensive? If the owners get a lot so should the players. Who made that rule? That segue only play well if you are a player. You're still only an employee. Even if I disagree, it's like the worker bee saying he/she should make what the CEO makes. Right or wrong, you just have to be at least consistent. The big thing is no one should be paid so much when people are starving. The money should be used to help the poor. Salaries for a games player should not be higher than the country's leader, therefore, $300k cap.

Advocates say "with the right education, practically anyone can fill the role of fireman, doctor or teacher." That one of the dumbest things I have ever heard. Besides, what is really more valuable to society and shouldn't that count for something? Police officers, firefighters, and doctors save lives while risking their own. You have children in 3rd world countries working way harder than simply practicing their ball skills after school and on weekends. Lawyers and Doctors spend years in college and work hard. Then they spend their life saving lives or someone's liberty. Tell me again how a football player compares to that? "Our future depends on the education of our children. Nothing important depends on how many points some overpaid ball player scores. So why do we pay athletes, musicians and actors so much? It isn't like the pay is even close. People in the military leave their families at home to defend and protect the country knowing they may never return.

There is also the argument that athletes should be paid more because the odds of succeeding are smaller. What's that got to do with anything? What are the odds of a guy with a 90 IQ becoming a doctor? Actually, this might be a useful argument if used properly- the fact that so few make it to the top. I keep hearing that and yet I still see second rate players making $500,000 to one million a year to sit on the bench.

The excuses keep coming and keep getting more obtuse. How about "If a fan is willing to spend money on a player, then that player deserves that money. They've earned it." Pure unadulterated horse pucky! Just because the fan is stupid doesn't make it right. Maybe the fan should wise up. There is no fact backing up this line of illogical argument.

The justification is that athletes instill people with a feeling of relaxation and excitement. I'd just as soon watch porn.

Have you seen some of these fans in the stands? It's not clear which is the bigger spectacle, the fan or the player. That's all it really is, isn't it, a spectacle? Just like the Gladiators, the Christians and the lions. So, how about three square meals a day and the right to keep on living?

Were the games less interesting 50 years ago when the players were getting $100 per week?

Today's players are spoiled babies. All they care about is the money and what it buys- houses, cars, toys etc.

Ever hear of Jamarcus Russel, the former No. 1 overall pick in the '07 draft? He gets over 60 million, with $31 million guaranteed even if he never plays. I didn't think so. That because he is one of the biggest flops of all time. In any other job, if you don't perform, you're fired. Unless you're Carly Fiorina that is.

In 2014, LeBron James made over $60,000,000, Cristiano Ronaldo made almost $80,000,000, and Floyd Mayweather made $300,000,000 (mostly in one night) (Lemco, 2015). Any one of those salaries could feed all the children in a third world country

CHAPTER FOUR – ENTITLED CHEATERS

The Tax Issue: Going Offshore

There is no question that large corporations and the rich individuals are cheating the government faster than the government can cheat the little guy. The typical corporation, in spite of whining like crybabies that the United States has the highest corporate tax rate, generally pays a lower effective rate than the average middle-class family. That's because of all the loopholes.

It's kind of like the banks taking huge risks. If they win, they get to keep the obscene profits. If they lose, the government bails then out. What a country. With the corporations, if they lose money they get all kinds of breaks from the government and then when then make money they can use tax credits from previous years to offset. I suggest you take another look at the practice of allowing corporations to move either their headquarters or some subsidiary offshore to avoid paying U.S. taxes. The same scrutiny applies to extremely wealthy individuals who routinely place their money out of the reach of our government. Again, I don't know who is more guilty, the rich or the incompetent government. Don't kid yourself with any freedom to shelter or "pay where you earn" or other such nonsense propagated by the rich, it is trickery and cheating. They are robbing the other tax payers of needed funds to take care of business, infrastructure, etc. Besides, these crooks are using those facilities. If they don't like it here, let them leave.

AbbVie, the drug company, bought a foreign company and will renounce its citizenship. It will now invert (big American company becomes a subsidiary of a smaller foreign company). It will still be managed from Chicago and control 75% of the new company. But 20% ownership by the subsidiary is all that is needed to stick it to Uncle Sam and consequently you and me. Result: U.S. tax avoidance from 22% rate to 13%, a bit over $1.3 billion (Dickinson, 2014). Bear in mind, the 13% doesn't even go to the United States, it goes to Ireland, or wherever. So they are saving 11%, but you are losing 22%" (All the advantages of living and working in the good old USA but at no cost. When they don't pay, you do.

OK, if my Dad is a Senator, and I'm CEO of a giant drug company, how wrong is it for me to give up my U.S. corporate citizenship? All the while crying out what a patriot I am. This person and her corporation get most of their income from Medicare and Medicaid. Well, Heather Bresch is doing just that at Mylan, and she has most people conned into believing it's because the big, bad, United States is a meany and picking on her (Fournier, 2014). Boo Hoo. I don't see a problem at all, just take away every single United States contract she has and let her go. You don't like it here, go. But don't keep your headquarters here and enjoy the many other benefits of living here. Otherwise, that's called being a hypocrite who condemn the U.S. political system while gaming it.

For once there is a bipartisan agreement between the Republicans and Democrats. They agree that the large corporations are ripping you and me off. They also agree to not do very much about it. Wealth is buying the agenda it wants and blocking that which it doesn't. Money talks, and the large corporations can afford to bribe Congress with all the money they are not paying you and me.

Corporation profits are up and taxes are down. Whoop dee doo. How the hell can they sleep at night? I sure can't. Oh yeah, that's right, they're amoral and just don't give a damn. They are so clever.

This just keeps getting better and better. Even for the profits they do concede to pay, it gets deferred until "repatriated, just like a 401K. Oh goodie.

Here is an example of how this can work. Let's say a drug company sells its intellectual property rights to a shell company (a shill or a subsidiary) who then overcharges the company on every deal lessening the profit here as well as providing some tax breaks also. The money probably never left the United States, parked at one of your other big buddy's (major bank), where it can be used in any number of ways. If anyone were ever to scream, all they have to do is borrow against the funds and then use the money. Corporations like this trick. Think these numbers are trivial? In 2013 these reinvested foreign funds were around two trillion dollars, a sum larger than the GDP of Russia. Some of the corporations and their amounts are:

- Microsoft ($76 billion)
- Pfizer ($69 billion)
- ExxonMobil ($47 billion)
- Walmart ($22 billion)
- Phillip Morris ($20 billion)
- McDonald's ($16 billion)
- Caterpillar ($17 billion)
- General Electric—They have an effective tax rate of 4% and at last count had $110 billion squirreled away overseas

Source (Dickinson, 2014).

If there is ever any question in your mind as to why the corporate tax doesn't bring in as much as individual tax, this is the reason. In the 1950s the corporation share of Federal Revenue was 30%, now it's 10% (Dickinson, 2014).

I read recently that somehow, the effort by corporations to avoid taxes was so they could lower the prices to the consumer. How stupid can you be? They want to avoid taxes so they, the top executives can put more money in their pockets.

People love to whine, and corporations are people. In fact, there must be a Whining 101 course taught at Harvard. I believe it replaced their ethics course, if they ever had one. So much for the fact that 35% is a high corporate tax. Nobody pays it so what's it matter? Bob McIntyre of Citizens for Justice once said "that corporate cheating has followed the path taken by so many others. Keep doing something wrong, get others to do it also, and sooner or later it will seem to be right" (Dickinson, 2014).

Naturally, the tax dodgers try to justify their avoidance by laying the blame on others for our having a 35% tax rate for corporations. Sounds like the chicken or the egg, or the pot calling the kettle black, or the three monkeys- see no evil, speak no evil or hear no evil. Even though I do not condone out war and bully policy, if you must do it you have to figure a way to pay for it, and 35% taxes are the way. Would you be curious to know what Germany pays for their military expenses? I know it may be premature, but it sure looks like they learned their lesson.

No matter what you do, the government for all its really poor procedures, doesn't seem to be able to go head to head with the cadre of high paid accountants at the powerful corporations. As soon as the government passes a law to curb the corporate excesses, the corporations find a loophole. It is probably true that the government is somewhat inefficient, but the corporate world more than wins the race to the bottom by being corrupt, greedy and self-serving.

Words like "gleeful" are used when describing how corporate accountants react to the stupidity or incompetence of the government.

There is also the disturbing revolving door between the government and either Wall Street or a large corporation.

My favorite undeserving, Georgie Bush, the younger, actually rewarded the corporations with a tax repatriation holiday during which the corporations brought back over $300 billion, which was done with the supposition that more jobs would be created. The charge for this was 5% instead of the 35% established rate. The corporations immediately proceeded to slash 20,000 jobs. These guys are laughing all the way to the bank. We just made the rich even richer. Around the time this was initiated there was around $600 billion offshore. As of 2014 there is over $2 trillion (Dickinson, 2014). Time for another forgiveness holiday.

Georgie Porgie (Bush-II),-, also rigged the estate tax by substantially increasing the amount of tax-free money someone can pass on to his heirs—from $1 million in 2001 to $3.5 million in 2009. Isn't he a great example of what money can buy?) Not that The Obama administration did anything about it, choosing to keep it at $3.5 million. Such policy only benefits the rich (Williams, 2011).

Let us not forget that hedge fund managers are taxed at a rate of only 15% because they can call their income "capital gains." That's not much, less than what most of the middle class pays. On this issue the Democrats and Republicans give lip service to attempt to close the loophole, but both have always voted to keep it. Something to do with generous campaign donations?

If the government is not in bed with the corporations and not doing them favors, then they are backing down from any verbally tough stance they take during campaigning.

Leaving the Country Loopholes

Corporations aren't the only ones who enter the limelight, both for their devious cleverness and for their selfish attitudes. Rich individuals who avail themselves of all that is good in our country, don't want to pay even their fair share, let alone help out those less fortunate. I suppose this has been going on for centuries. Which, as opposed to business as usual, means it's time to do something about it.

In 2014 French actor Gérard Depardieu dramatically, as an actor would, wrote a letter to the French Prime Minister, saying he was unhappy, the government was being mean to him, and he was leaving. In the letter he opined that governments think success, creation, talent, and anything different should be punished. (Sayare, 2012) Typical one-sided self-justification. I don't recall anyone ever saying it was a punishment, merely a tax because you have been privileged to lead a great life, far above your merit in most cases, and should pay for that. This was brought on by the President's recent tax hike on the upper levels to 75%. (Ruitenberg, 2013)You know, 25% of an obscene amount is still pretty good and probably still many factors what everyone else is making. I think France should levy a special tax on Depardieu just for spite and to teach others a lesson.

No question Belgium should not accept him, however. They can have any tax system they want as long as they can make ends meet. But don't ask for any handouts and don't give sanctuary.

Who to blame more, the narcissistic ego maniacs in government or the narcissistic greedy ego maniacs who make movies for a living?

I'm rummaging through my notes, trying to determine what, if anything, some movie star has contributed to the well-being of a nation. I even liked the guy as an actor. I like chocolate candy, but I can do without, and it doesn't affect my livelihood.

The Top One Percent

You're not going to believe this, but, there are those who whine that even the top one percent are getting screwed by the top one tenth of a percent. No doubt that's true but the question is, who cares? Poor babies who are making a minimum of around $350,000 as of 2009 and up to a little less than a million. Not that anyone has any sympathy for any of them. Can you imagine after the rip off perpetrated in the last five years, or so, how bad it must be now?

The top 1 percent is supposedly misleading because it combines those making the above mentioned $350,000 with the gazillionaires making 100 million a year. Some make a billion. If you're not rolling in the isles by now at this sub story, shame on you. Uncle Sam exacerbated this misconception because the IRS does not break down income bracket any further than the top one percent. Emmanuel Saez, a University of California economist famous for writing with Thomas Piketty, has broken out the top one tenth of one percent. (Johnson D. C., 2011). Saez got his information from tax records. Seems pretty reliable.

"All we ever hear from the Republican rich is how around half the people don't pay any taxes and the top one percent pay around 37%." (Johnson D. C., 2011) I wouldn't get too hung up on the 37%, the number can fluctuate somewhat depending on the study. Not really important. Even so, those numbers are extremely misleading. Let's turn that statement around. Naturally that half doesn't pay any income tax, they don't make any money and are starving. Twenty percent of nothing is still nothing. Doesn't anyone think it sad that around half of the people in the country are in the lowest tax bracket? The raw net amount left after taxes is what's important and it's so much greater for the rich. When you crank up the numbers to include those citizens making up to 75,000 dollars, this collective group now pay more in taxes than the group making over one million dollars. Put another way, "those in the 15% bracket pay more than those in the top 2%. The fact is that the government relies far more on the bottom 99 percent than the top 1 percent for federal income taxes." (Johnson D. C.) To add injury to insult, after all that, the top one tenth of one percent pay the lowest tax rates.

Johnson then stepped out of his decency robe once and stated that "a big difference between the top tenth and the bottom poverty stricken of the one per-centers had to go to work every day. (Johnson D. C., 2011) Gee, I thought that what's the puritan religious ethic taught us to do? Like the rest of don't?

The median income taxpayer — half made more, half less — made slightly less than $33,000 in 2008. After adjustments that comes out to around $300 per week. (Johnson D. C., 2011) Again, maybe $33,000 is subject to some adjustment but that's not the point. If you think someone making 300 times the average worker's pay should be shot, how does 30,000 grab you? That means it would take you 30,000 years to make that kind of money.

CHAPTER FIVE - FALLACIES IN THAT LOGIC

The Rich Don't Create Jobs

Henry Blodgett said, "it is assumed to be fact that rich people create the jobs. Specifically, entrepreneurs and investors, when given low taxes or tax breaks, build companies and create millions of jobs. And these entrepreneurs and investors, therefore, the argument goes, can solve our nation's huge unemployment problem—if only we cut taxes and regulations so they can have more incentive to build more companies and create more jobs." (Blodget, 2011)

In other words, by even considering raising taxes on "The 1%," we are considering destroying the very mechanism that makes our economy the strongest and biggest in the world: The incentive for entrepreneurs and investors to build companies in the hope of getting rich and, in the process, creating millions of jobs. Obviously after 40 years of tax cuts on the rich and an increasing wealth differential everyone should be convinced tax cuts on the rich just do not work and are wrong.

Taxes on rich people (capital gains and income) are, relative to history, low; so raising them would only begin to bring them back in line with prior prosperous periods, plus dozens of rich entrepreneurs have already gone on record confirming that a modest hike in capital gains and income taxes would not have the slightest impact on their desire to create companies and jobs, given that tax rates are historically low.

"The theory that 'rich people create the jobs' is absurd," argues Nick Hannauer, the founder of online advertising company aQuantive. You remember Nick, he's the guy we spoke of in the introduction, who says the rich should do something, all the while tooting his own horn. I am curious as to the motivation of these rich guys, espousing more for the poor- after they're squirreled theirs away. Which would be the better description, arrogance or hubris? "Even if they found and build companies that eventually employ thousands of people, what creates the jobs starts with the company's customers who buy the company's products, which, in turn, creates the need for the employees to produce, sell, and service those products. If those customers go broke or simply don't have enough money, the demand for the company's products will collapse. Then the jobs will disappear, regardless of what the entrepreneur does. Not that entrepreneurs are not an important part of the equation. So are investors, who risk capital. But, ultimately, whether a new company continues growing and creating jobs is a function of having customers and their ability and willingness to pay for the company's products, not the entrepreneur or the investor capital." (Blodget, 2011).

So, who are these customers? And what can government policy do to make sure these customers have more money to spend to create demand and, thus, jobs? The customers of most companies are still mostly the middle class—the hundreds of millions of Americans who currently take home a much smaller share of the national income than they did 30 years ago, before tax policy aimed at helping rich people get richer created the greatest income and wealth inequality since the 1920s. We all know where that led, right? The middle class can't even get a tax break, the rich get that also. All of this assumes there will still be a middle class left in a few more years. Who would that be anyway? A family with a child or two struggles on $60,000 per year. Yet, where do you get that kind of money?   Isn't the money paid to the rich 1% supposed to 'trickle down' to the middle class and thus benefit everyone? Isn't that the way it's supposed to work? Unfortunately, that's not the way it actually works. This is how it really works: Hanauer takes home more than $10 million a year of income. On this income, he says, he pays an 11% tax rate." (Blodget, 2011) This 'trickle down' garbage has been around since the Reagan administration. "With the approximately $9 million a year Hanauer keeps, he buys lots of stuff. But, importantly, he doesn't buy as much stuff as would be bought if that $9 million were instead earned by 9,000 U.S. citizens each taking home an extra $1,000 a year. Why not? Because, despite Hanauer's impressive lifestyle, most of the $9+ million just goes straight into the bank (where it either sits and earns interest or gets invested in companies that ultimately need strong demand to sell products and create jobs). Hanauer points out that his family owns 3 cars, not the 3,000 that might be bought if his $9+ million were taken home by a few thousand families. How about a house? No matter how big, give him credit for a big house and a second home in Aspen at $10 million each. Three thousand times $150,000 is $450 million versus the $20 million above. No contest. Multiply that by every other item in an average budget and you can see the buying power we are losing and therefore, the job creation. Hanauer reiterated the theme so often espoused here, that most American families haven't improved their standard of living since the 1970s.

The Result of This Obscene Pay?

"Companies with the highest paid CEOs are actually poorer performers. In a study of 1,500 companies with the largest market values, the 10% with the highest-paid CEOs under-performed their peers by a margin of about 11% over a three-year period. The more CEOs are paid, the worse the firm does over the following three years. Thirty years ago, the average CEO made 46 times the pay of the average worker. Now they make 331 times more (Simkins, 2014).

Here are a few more examples of why you are getting left behind. Even as recently as the Enron scandals, somebody went to prison. Fast forward to the 2007 debacle. "Merrill Lynch revealed a $7.9 billion loss on sub-prime bets in 2007, they fired their CEO, Stanley O'Neal, and gave him *$161.5 million* as he exited. Ex-Citigroup CEO Chuck Prince, walked with $140 million while scratching his head as to where they had lost the money." (Smith R. , 2007) None of this helped the stock either. Would this be a good place to remind you that a mere 3–5% drop in assets at the astounding leverage these guys are using would make them bankrupt. I could go on and on.

Morgan Stanley, J.P. Morgan, Bank of America, Bear Sterns, Goldman Sachs, etc. These corporations are made up of people you wouldn't want to turn your back on, or have over to a barbecue. Lest we forget, the dual edged sword used by these guys/gals is paying big bonuses while laying off thousands of employees. And they're laughing at us all the while. They really believe they are better than we are. Perhaps they're right in an academic sense. Should we feel OK about being dumped on? Don't think it's just CEOs; the rant includes entertainers and sports figures also, who generally are not better than we are, especially academically. If you are OK with paying millions of dollars a year to someone to play a game, shame on you. We need to determine what kind of

world we want to live in and what standards one uses
to judge the worth of a human being.

CHAPTER SIX - THE ACTUAL NUMBERS

Averages

Repeating that liars figure and figures lie, let's visit with the term "averages". The "average" American worker earns about $44,000 per year and saves around 4% of his income. And the "average" household has a net worth of $710,000, including the value of homes, investments, bank accounts, and so on. (Newman, 2014) Are you kidding me? When was the last time you saw $710,000? Wanna know how that can be? Easy. Averages can be distorted by a few very large numbers at the top (or bottom for that matter).

According to your lying, cheating, backbiting government the economy is gaining strength. So how come millions of ordinary people feel like they're falling behind? Not only that but also because the rich have a lot more discretionary income they can save a lot more also, without even breaking stride. Which means not only does their huge amount at 4% really skew the averages, but also they actually save a bigger percentage than 4. "The normal wealthy save about 12% of their income and the richest 1% save 38% of their income." (Samurai, 2015)

As for the bottom 90% of earners, for a decade prior to the 2007 recession, the savings rate for this group was negative. (Samurai, 2015) I seriously bet the government throws out those years as being outliers.

One of the reasons for the widening gap is that the two biggest wealth builders, home equity and the stock market—are assets held primarily by the rich. Both these wealth builders are declining for the average consumer. As opposed to the silly average stated above, a *Forbes* survey from around 2008 stated, "The bottom 80% of American earners have a net worth of around only $82,000, with many folks stuck with a negative net worth. (Holland, 2006) Much more believable.

According to *Forbes*, the wealthiest 400 Americans' average net worth was $3.9 billion in 2008—more than six times larger than it was in 1985.

This discussion addresses the assets of the average household, but it applies equally to the income also. See Appendix C

Why leave out the housing market figures? It's the same travesty. Houses sold to the top 1% of households, volume was up by 20–100% in most markets. By contrast, transaction volume during that same period was down for the entire remaining 99% of the market in 26 out of 30 cities. (Stockman, 2014)

Actual CEO Pay

"The top 0.01% of Americans now individually earns more than $35 million a year. They earn $1 out of every

$17—the group's highest amount since data collection began in 1913." (Williams, 2011)

"CEOs on Business Week's Executive Pay Scoreboard of 365 major U.S. companies hauled in an average $8.1 million in 2003—up 9 percent from 2002—including salary, bonus, and long-term compensation such as restricted stock and exercised stock options. That's more than $22,000 every day of the year. The average full-time production and non-supervisory worker made $31,928 in 2003 and $31,769 in 1980, adjusted for inflation—a gain of $159. CEO pay skyrocketed 480 percent during 1980–2003, adjusted for inflation, while domestic corporate profits rose 145 percent, worker productivity rose 61 percent and worker pay stalled. If CEO and worker pay had increased at the pace of worker productivity, CEOs would have made $2.3 million in 2003 and workers $51,148. CEOs made 44 times as much as workers in 1980; by 1990, the ratio was 107. In 2008 top executives averaged $10.8 million in total compensation, over 364 times the pay of the average American worker," (Pizzigati, 2007). CEOs in the United States are paid like kings.

"Average CEO pay was $11.4 million in 2010, then rose to $12.9 million in 2011." (Liberto, 2012) How much did your pay increase over that period?

Defenders of this recent increase in pay think it is largely the result of a healthy stock market and also that a large majority of shareholders who want to avoid losing money with poorly performing executives, approve of how much their companies' CEOs are making. Shear horse pucky. Haven't you noticed, the CEOs get the big pay even when companies do poorly? How do you tell up front who will perform poorly?

"Pay to be tied to performance is becoming more of a trend," says Kevin Scott, co-founder/CEO of the ADDO Institute, "And now, as their stocks are performing at very high levels, those CEOs are reaping the benefits." (Mishel & Davis, 2015) Tied to performance but at a lesser rate so they only make $300,000. He is a CEO so his opinion is tainted from the start and should not be considered. If you think there is any chance whatsoever of shareholders votes making a difference you're smoking something, and it's not tobacco. Scott also thinks that non-shareholders shouldn't be telling boards how much a CEO is worth. Maybe, maybe not.

When the *Wall Street Journal* says companies' boards have responded to this regulation, and are basing CEO compensation on how well a company is doing, I feel the need to look over my shoulder. How many times will we be willing to believe this dribble? The only time these people respond to anything is when they are backed into a corner or else believe it will do them some good.

Chicago's Booth professor Steven Neil Kaplan believes "CEOs pay packages are not the result of greed and excess, and argues that CEO pay should be compared with the salaries of other high-earning professionals: "If you look at CEO pay compared to the average pay of people in the top 0.1%, it's about where it was 20 years ago—in line with that of lawyers and private-company executives, and less than hedge-fund managers." (Feloni, 2014) Another result of picking and choosing your information source. Two wrongs do not make a right. All of them, along with the athletes, musicians, and actors should be grateful to live in the United States and settle for the token $300,000.

"The *Wall Street Journal* stated that in a survey taken of the Russell 3000 Index companies, 93% approved of their CEO's pay." (Lomax, 2014) Huh. I guess that makes three wrongs. It failed to mention who they surveyed, the company shareholders, managers, or employees and if the CEO was in the room at the time.

Gap Disparity

One of the hardest things to determine is who is lying and who is telling the truth. Usually research based information has more credibility. With that in mind, it behooves us to load you up with more actual examples of the ridiculous inequality. I never tire of saying, "no one is worth this much more than the rest of us." "Equilar, the compensation analytics firm in Redwood City, Calif., who in turn got much of their data from figures from a program of the Bureau of Labor Statistics, found that the median package was $14.3 million for 2014." (Baker, 2013) Mr. Baker and others readily admit there is also a wide gap as to what the average worker makes. That average includes government spending, not just what workers earn.

The following numbers were obtained by the Center for Economic and Policy Research:

The company with the widest pay gap on the list was Walt Disney, whose chief executive, Robert Iger, received $43.7 million. Given Mr. Baker's estimate that Disney's median worker received $19,530, that translates to a C.E.O. multiple of 2,238 to one. Second on the list was Satya Nadella, Microsoft's chief. His pay package of $84.3 million last year placed him at 2,012 times the estimate of $41,900 for the median employee's earnings at Microsoft. Oracle's founder, Lawrence J. Ellison, ranks third on the pay gap list: 1,183 to one by Mr. Baker's calculations. Next up was Steven M. Mollenkopf, chief executive of Qualcomm, whose $60.7 million in compensation puts him at 1,111 times the median worker estimate at the San Diego Company, which makes wireless telecommunication equipment and software. Howard D. Schultz, founder and chief executive of Starbucks, ranked fifth. He received $21.5 million last year, or 1,073 times the typical barista's salary. (Morgenson, 2015)

There is always another side to the story, twisted and full of holes as it may be. Here are a few lines of dribble from company spokesmen:

- "A Disney spokesman said that 92 percent of Mr. Iger's compensation was based on the company's financial performance, which was outstanding in 2014. A Microsoft spokesman disputed the calculation, saying that a typical employee at the company earned "well north of $100,000," and that much of Mr. Nadella's pay would be realized only in coming years — if the company performed well. He contended that a better measure of Mr. Nadella's pay for 2014 was $22.75 million. Using Microsoft's figures, Mr. Nadella's pay ratio would still be at least 150 to one. A Qualcomm spokeswoman said only $28.7 million of Mr. Mollenkopf's package should be used for a pay comparison. This would lower his ratio to 526 to 1. A company spokeswoman said its executive compensation was linked to company performance, 'and our board has determined that Howard Schultz's pay reflects both competitive considerations and value to the company.' She added that lower-level workers receive a wide array of benefits in addition to their salaries." A Honeywell spokesman said "more than 90 percent of our C.E.O.'s pay is variable, at-risk and long term," emphasizing profit growth and stock appreciation. Which inflation pretty much guarantees will go up, right? An AT&T spokesman said 92 percent of the C.E.O.'s target compensation was tied to company performance, including stock price. There must be some basis, otherwise how were the studies able to come up with the ratios? What was it based on? (Morgenson, 2015)

"These C.E.O.s are smart, hard-working people," Mr. Baker said. "But there is no basis for believing that if companies don't pay $84 million they won't attract top talent. You go back 40 years and they had smart, hard-working people too. (Morgenson, 2015) Besides, I know a lot of hardworking people who make $12 per hour.

No one is saying that CEOs shouldn't be rewarded if the company does well, just not that well. Simple solution- make the compensation ratio smaller.

One of the reasons top executives get away with this is that, in spite of government rulings (the Dodd-Frank law of 2010) stating that the corporations are supposed to provide the gap, it's almost impossible for the average person to wade through the mounds of corporate filings to try and find the information. Of course, one shouldn't have to. A sub reason you can't find the information is that lobbyists have stonewalled the Securities and Exchange Commission on their efforts to enforce Dodd-Frank.

Another amusing fact garnered from this particular article, although by no means exclusive to it, is that it is information from Gretchen Morgenstern, taken from the Center for Economic and Policy Research, who took it from Equilar, who got it from the government Bureau of Statistics. It's no wonder information isn't correct. I also don't have a clue how to cite that.

Whenever something goes parabolic (going higher and higher faster and faster, as in this wage gap- or spending of money you don't have for that matter) there is probably an unpleasant ending.

CHAPTER SEVEN - OTHER ISSUES

Minimum Wage

Forget that there hasn't been an increase in the minimum wage in a number of years and minimum wage isn't anywhere near as high compared to other wages as it has been in the past. More to the point would be why? In 2014 Congress debated an increase to $10.10. Had that gone through it would have only put the ratios back to where they were in the late 1960s. If minimum wages had kept up with inflation it would be at $18 per hour. It seems pretty important to differentiate between these two figures. Just getting the equivalent of what workers got in 1960 isn't the same as staying even with inflation. It hasn't been raised for over a decade. If one uses the productivity growth as a benchmark rather than inflation, which make sense also, the minimum wage would have reached $21.72 per hour in 2012. Either is a reasonable benchmark if you have any wish to have fairness be a factor in your society. This looks like another good place for a rant. Make your choice. If you are happy with the cave man mentality and your intent is not to improve society, then you should not have a place setting at the table of reasonable people. If, however, you do feel we should strive to improve our lot, then fairness is a big part of your plan. And fairness means reducing the inequality gap. Don't harken back to other time periods and say, "well, they did it." Most of us stopped using that logic when we were nine. Ever wonder how that compares to the gross pay increases for upper management and talent? I thought you'd never ask.

American CEO's are the highest paid in the world. As of 2011, Corporate CEO's in America make *340 times* what the average worker makes. As a comparison, in 1980, CEO pay was only 42 times more than the average worker. (Nader, 2013) The minimum wage, from $5.15, increased to $5.85 in July, 2007, $6.55 in July, 2008, and to $7.25 in July 2009. A minimum wage at the $5.15 rate equals $10,300 a year. I was making more than that as an entry level employee at IBM back in 1969. "Before that it had been ten years since it had been raised. In 1968, the minimum wage was $1.60. That's $10.71 in 2013 dollars." (Nader, 2013) Even according to the Bureau of Statistics CEOs at big companies earned 110 times the 2005 average household income, which was $58,700." (Nader, 2013) Need we reiterate that the government lies? The Heritage Foundation, an acknowledged republican stronghold, even stated that the minimum wage was $8.67 in 1968. (Sherk, 2013) A study by Oregon State University used the very same Department of Labor statistics and somehow came up with $10.60 in 1968. Who do you believe? It doesn't really matter, they both illustrate that minimum wage isn't high enough. The rich conservatives insist that minimum wage positions are supposedly learning wage positions—they enable workers to gain the skills necessary to become more productive on the job. Go for it Pinocchio. As workers become more productive they command higher pay and move up their career ladder. If only that were true. Two-thirds of minimum wage workers earn a raise within a year. Raising the minimum wage makes such entry-level positions less available." (Sherk, 2013) To be honest, as discussed previously, the statement that the average income earner earns $58,000 per year is ridiculous. To repeat, averages are skewed upward by the huge numbers at the top so the number doesn't mean anything. Now the 42 times mentioned above is over 350 times. (Nader, 2013) I would dearly love to know if there is a conspiracy or these people just don't get it right.

The spread between the wealthy and the poor is increasingly more like that in a third-world country. Graft and corruption in government and business must surely be at an all-time high. Huge disparities exist between the salaries of those at the top of major corporations and those in the trenches. Has it always been this way? It doesn't matter. That's why we read Charles Dickens; to learn from the past and our mistakes. But at least these businessmen/women appear to be doing something productive. Are we sure that we can't balance the budget by simply capping our talent industries at a reasonable figure (say $300,000 a year) and apply the rest to the deficit. Yeah, it would probably take a long time to break even—like a year or two.

In his letter to Mike Duke, CEO of Walmart (who makes $11,000 per hour), Ralph Nader said, "Raising your workers' wages to a $10.50 minimum would cost your company less than $2 billion (deductible) on U.S. sales of more than $313 billion. Fewer Walmart workers would have to go on various forms of government relief. Some of that $2 billion would go to social security and Medicare, with more going back into purchases at Walmart. Employee turnover would diminish. Sadly Nader went on to say if Walmart joined with many civic, charitable groups and unions to press Congress for legislation to catch up with 1968 for 30 million American workers, good things will happen. You and your fellow executives will feel better." (Nader, 2013) Really Ralph, feel better? Stephen Gandel makes the case that Walmart should give its employees a 50% raise. According to him, the company is misallocating capital by not paying higher wages. He says investors are not giving the company credit for the lower pay in the stock price, so they should just do the right thing and pay their employees more. (French, Minimum Wage, Maximum Stupidity, 2014) How do we know that low wages have anything to do with as low stock price? French went on to say, "Whatever Walmart is paying, it must be enough, because it has plenty of applicants to choose from. In 2005, 11,000 people in the San Francisco Bay Area applied for 400 positions at a new Oakland store.

Three years later near Chicago, 25,000 people applied for 325 positions at a new store." (French, Minimum Wage, Maximum Stupidity) All twisted logic. Again, why give Walmart credit for the fact that there are simply not enough decent jobs?

These overpaid people believe they are entitled to everything and accountable to no one. They also believe they have done nothing wrong. Nader calls the inequality gap a runaway train. He also said it should not be called Income Inequality but rather Income Tyranny. To really put frosting on the cake, these outrageous pay increases not only didn't stop during the hard times from 2007 through 2011, the actually increased. How can that be?

All cuts in wages do not pass through to customers. Why reduce the living wage of the average worker just to line the pockets of upper management? Looking at Cosco would dispel the theory that, if a business pays more than the market wage rate, the business "would be in trouble financially. The rich say if you pay less than the market, employees leave to work somewhere else. Maybe, except there is nowhere else to go—monopolies, oligarchies, cabals and cartels see to that.

Those in positions of power have profited off the backs of the working poor for thousands of years.

Nick Dearden, director of Global Justice Now worries that we have no plan on how to solve this dilemma. Large Trans-National corporations and their power is fundamental to the staggering levels of inequality which afflict the world, and are also quite prepared to destroy the planet in their greedy quest for ever more profit. The problem of poverty is inseparable from the problem of super-wealth; Exploitation and the monopolization of resources by the few is the cause of poverty. (Germanos, 2015)

The minimum wage issue is a distraction that could be eliminated entirely by reducing the gap between the high pay for those at the top and the rest of us. It isn't that those at the bottom are paid too little, it's that those at the top are paid too much.

Fast Foods

The recent fast food industry attempt to increase their minimum wage to $15 once again asked the question, "Would granting that kind of minimum wage result in layoffs? The study by Robert Pollin and Jeannette Wicks-Lim of the University of Massachusetts-Amherst says no. They found that the extra cost would be countered by, a slight increase in prices (offset by a reduction in sales- 3% versus 1.5%), reduced turnover and an increase in efficiency because workers are happier, and greater economic growth which would track with the economy's growth, estimated at 2.5%, presumably occurring because people would have more money and spend it. (Covert, 2013).

A full-time worker who sees her pay go from $7.25 an hour ($15,000 per year) to $15 an hour ($30,000 per year) will have another $15,000 to spend each year. This can go to hire childcare for her children, home health care workers for parents, or be spent in thousands of other ways. The higher minimum wage can actually increase employment, owing to additional "money in the pockets" of workers that they will spend in the economy, which in turn causes greater demand for goods and services--- and more employment for workers (Widmaier, 2013). That's economic growth.

There is also the effect on those already making more than minimum wage. You know, "If he gets more, I should get more." The U. Mass. study was thorough enough to take into consideration not only the minimum wage increase but some increase for those above that in order to maintain status quo. The study estimated that in an industry that generates $232 billion dollars the cost would be $30 billion, a 15% cost increase. The study also uncovered the fact that many companies are smart enough to realize that laying off workers impairs growth or the ability to be ready for growth possibilities when they come. Sadly the companies also would do anything rather than cut their profits so there is a bit of conflict there. (Covert, 2013)

That 15% gets whittled down somewhat too, because of those above mentioned offsets. According to the study, reduced turnover alone would reduce the cost by 20%. Fast food restaurants experience a turnover rate of 120 percent, and it costs $4,700 for each worker who leaves. (Covert, 2013)

Given a very modest reduction in profits, a pay reduction for top executives, more efficiency, and savings on turnover, prices might still have to increase very little. A Big Mac that used to cost $4.00 will now cost $4.20. How many people do you think that will stop from buying? Not many. That's probably the worst case scenario. In spite of the Congressional Budget Office (Liars?) saying there will be job losses; based on the above, if you put all of those savings together the companies actually make money on the deal and no one loses any jobs. In fact, States with higher minimum wages experienced above average job growth. (Covert, 2013).

"A $10.10 wage then means a savings from reduced turnover of $2.1 billion, or 28 percent of the cost of the raise, and a $15 wage means $5.2 billion in savings, or 17 percent of the costs." (Covert, 2013). You can see where there is a lot of room for manipulation of data as the numbers inch up or down.

A study from 2011 found that raising wages at big box stores to $12 an hour would raise their labor costs by around 10 percent. Estimating that number for $15/hour should raise labor costs 20% being very conservative. If labor costs are 30 percent of the total costs at fast food chains (the rest going for the food, rent, utilities, etc), multiply the 20% times the 30% and you get 6% of the total cost. That study also corroborated the fact that higher pay is associated with sharp reductions in turnover, which means lower costs for employers. (Baker, 2013)

If you throw in the possibility that the companies might even reduce their profits a little bit more than 1% (which are currently at record highs—boo hoo), this is becoming a real bonanza. Heaven forbid the hogs at the top chip in.

Whether spreading around the wealth by everyone taking a small cut in pay is better or worse than losing a small percentage of jobs while making more money for those working is a difficult quandary to resolve. The easy solution is to take money from the CEOs and create more and higher paying jobs.

When did minimum wage become an issue? Either thank (or crucify) FDR for that. Lots of social programs came into being then. Obviously, there was a problem of some sort. Roosevelt's Fair Labor Standards Act of 1938 banned oppressive child labor as well as guaranteeing a minimum hourly wage of 25 cents. What's not to like? Yet even the Supreme Court hated it, asking why the federal government was mingling with the affairs of private businesses. The court argued that the law was unconstitutional even. Any discussion of the Supreme Court will quickly let you know they are not immune to lining up politically on any topic- liberals versus conservative.

It isn't like American businesses or their CEOs can't afford to help out the less fortunate. Yet whining about minimum wages takes center stage. The system is broken. When CEOs are raking in salaries that are hundreds, if not thousands, of times larger than their low-level workers, something is wrong. And the fact that not enough people are concerned about it makes things even more wrong. I suppose people are afraid they will lose their jobs and things will get even worse.

In an ideal world we would raise low-level employee wages and force top executives to rethink their huge profit-grabbing salaries. If shareholders stand up for their rights as true owners of a company, corporate profits would remain high and unnecessarily large executive salaries would be cut. Blah, blah, blah. Unfortunately, that ain't going to happen. The only thing amoral people understand is force, since they both don't understand someone else's plight or simply don't care. We will have to make an example of some of them.

Australia paid $16.37 per hour minimum wage in 2012 and had unemployment of 5.6%. (Noor, 2013). Yes, these numbers may need to be adjusted for parity. Parity meaning making sure the numbers mean the same thing by comparing the cost of a loaf of bread in each country. As of this writing, (2015) the US dollar has strengthens against the Australian dollar, but in 2013 when this study was conducted parity wasn't a factor since the ratio ranged from .90 Australian dollars to the US dollar to 1.05 Australian dollars to the US dollar. About the same. The unemployment number from Australia was 5.6% when the number in the United States was 7.5%. (No adjustment necessary.) Depending on whose figures you believe, the $16.37 or $16.88 dollar rate when adjusted goes to an American dollar at $15 and change if the Australian dollar were at the low end of the conversion rate (90%). It was not within the scope of this book to verify these numbers. Ceteris paribus (all other things being equal) applies here. Speaking of which, the Australian study was criticized for who they did and did not include in the study. A valid concern. The only problem is, we pick and choose our numbers here in the United States also. As to this concern, it has to do with those who are not working a full 40-hour week and would like to do so. Our numbers in the United States suggest that all the percentages would at least double if those people were included in the unemployment rolls. As mentioned in another section, to be fair; perhaps a percentage of their numbers should be included, sort of a half unemployed person if you will. Makes sense.

Australia is merely one example of those countries who seem to manage to not destroy their population as we do here in the United States. Many other countries have decent minimum wages. A minimum wage of $10 is still only $20,000 per year. That's still poverty in most advanced western countries. The rich would have you believe there is something to the fact that some of the better countries don't even have minimum wages at all. That fails to take into consideration that these countries, such as Denmark, Germany, Italy, Norway, Singapore, Sweden, and Switzerland, have strong unions who participate in collective bargaining, which keeps wages in line automatically. (Matthews, 2013) Read any newspaper (old school) and you will know that every one of these countries not only pays everyone well but is at the top of every one's wish list as a place to live. Swiss voters voted down a 22-franc (nearly $25) minimum wage in early 2014 (May). 76% voted to reject what would have been the world's highest minimum wage. Why would they do that? As much respect for the Swiss as I have, I am relieved to know they are not perfect either. For perspective, a one bedroom flat in a large city in Switzerland costs around $2100 per month. Of course, with Germany paying 8.5 ($9.30) euros per hour minimum wage, the Swiss are already way above that. (French, Minimum Wage, Maximum Stupidity, 2014) Although not necessarily tied directly to minimum wage, it may be useful to know the average wage in several European countries. Here are the top several:

Salaries and Minimum Wage

	Avg. Wage	Minimum-wage
Liechtenstein	not even listed it so high!	
Switzerland	$6407	none
Denmark	$5970	none
Norway	$5632	none
Luxembourg	$5864	2411
Ireland	$5423	2056
Germany	3703	none
Netherlands	4675	1974
Belgium	4428	2055
Austria	4235	1371
Finland	4202	none
UK	3930	1605
France	4001	1872
Sweden	3600	none
Italy	3200	none
Spain	3000	880

Source: United Nations Economic Commission for Europe, Federation of European Employees, United Nations Statistics Division

   In spite of varying results, you can begin to see a pattern as several names become repeaters on all lists.

After seeing a country on several lists in approximately the same position one can have some comfort that those numbers are at least close.

The tax rate does play a part. The problem is one usually doesn't know what, such as health care, education, public transportation or retirement pension, is included free to the consumer and the quality of that service. We also never know exactly what deductions are available from that tax base. This where the United States shines. We are the masters of loopholes.

An additional chart to include tax rates:

CTRY	Hours/wk	Tax rate
US	40 hrs	23%
Ireland		18.9%
Luxembourg		28-37%
Switzerland	35 hrs	30%
Australia	35 hrs	23-27%
England	42 hrs	25-50%
Canada	34 hrs	23-31%
Germany		49.8%
Austria		49.4%
Norway-	32 hrs	37%
Netherlands	35 hrs	38-52%
Sweden		56.6%
France	35 hrs	49.4%
South Korea	45 hrs	12%

Source: the richest.com

As one can see, even these two lists do not correspond. In fact, the second list is a compilation of several. The exercise is to take a look at the United States, decide how things are going for us, and maybe get some ideas on how to improve. If you think the average wage in the United States is a net of $42,000 I want what you've been smoking.

Like other countries, numerous states also have higher minimum wages than the Federal Government. Why do the states feel it necessary to do this if there are those who believe we shouldn't even have a minimum wage?

The Australian system as well as many others (with the exception of the United States) , not only provides for a decent minimum wage but also workers have, sick days, four weeks annual leave, educational assistance, transportation assistance and full health insurance. The French and the Germans get six weeks' vacation.

Finally there is the prospect of a sliding scale for the minimum wage, for example, less for teenagers. Why don't we at least do this here in the United States? In Australia there is a sliding scale for youth workers based on the full benefit in force at the time. For example, If the minimum wage is $16.87 per hour and you are under 16 you get 36.8% of the full $16.87, at 16 you get 47.3%, 17 is 57.8, 18 is 68.3%, 19 is 82.5% and 20 is 97.7%. (Noor, 2013) All in all a reasonable solution. As to why an eighteen year old is old enough to go to war, vote and drive but can't get full pay is another matter. Perhaps rather than paying them less we should consider not sending them to war. That notwithstanding, no matter what fairy tale world you live in, there is no doubt that the work habits of a 16 year old are not as good as someone older. To be honest I can see where some people might argue for the sliding scale to reach all the way up into the twenties.

Democrats call Republicans heartless for dismissing vulnerable workers for whom the federal minimum wage has not increased from $7.25 since 2009. Republicans accuse Democrats of brutalizing the business environment at a time of painful unemployment. The latest poll from Reason-Rupe says 67% of Americans favor an increase in the minimum to $10.10 per hour from $7.25. (Miller D. , 2014). According to a recent Gallup poll, over 70 percent of the American public support raising the minimum wage. Many economists agree that it would stimulate the economy through larger sales volume, not harm it. (Nader, 2013) Supporters of a higher minimum wage are citing a report by the Center for Economic and Policy Research (CEPR) as evidence that raising the minimum wage really doesn't kill jobs (Schmitt, 2013). Since we have studies from both sides of the argument I guess we'll have to flip a coin. There is plenty of evidence that most studies are usually skewed or biased, written with an agenda; or the statistical difference is so minuscule as to not be important.

Those advocating a higher minimum wage argue there's an obvious option: Share those profits more equitably with employees through higher wages and, thus, reduced profits for the capitalists. Rumors again say redirecting profits into greater employee pay reduces a company's competitiveness in a globalized world. I wonder. But it's OK to pay themselves more. That called circuitous logic. Or greed. You choose. How can they say they are competitive yet make more profit? The profit going instead to workers would have nothing to do with competitiveness, just reduce profit. Lifting wages might reduce profit margins or it might require consumer costs to rise so that margins are maintained. Or we could just take the money from the CEOs and the profit margin would not change.

Should the government step in and do something? Left to their own devices, corporations will run rough shod over workers.

Productivity is one of the measures of who is losing their job. Since more work falls on the backs of those left behind and they are forced to worker harder, productivity increases on the books. Therefore, higher productivity can very often mean fewer jobs. A great justification for getting rid of employees if you are a CEO seeking to maximize your own pay and bonus.

Regarding the tie in between minimum wage and unemployment, this is some of the ridiculous and self-serving logic we hear. A Labor Department report once said, "A part of the increase you are seeing in unemployment is attributable to temporary layoffs in the auto industry," and these layoffs accounted for, according to him, "a significant portion" of the rise in the number of filings. (Epstein, 2005) They always have an excuse. I am sure that the people laid off from the auto industry feel a lot better knowing that! My guess is that when these temps go back to work the pencil pushers will not miss a beat in taking credit for that without any footnotes that they were temporarily laid off in the first place. Also gains reported are assisted by making assumptions of people getting work that has no basis in fact. Just government mumbo jumbo. I wonder how much validity the current unemployment figures have.

Another problem. The minimum wage doesn't affect anyone working in the insurance business, oil business, utility business, etc. See? The minimum wage only effects a small portion of the economy. That also means you don't have the attentive ear of those industries that are unaffected.

It doesn't matter how you slice it, $20,000 per year versus $10,000,000 for some CEO has flaws. That's 500 times as much! We are talking about the United States here. And please don't cry for even the small business person. They are doing just fine. Raising the minimum wage would just be a drop in the bucket and merely a good place to start.

It is a little hard to sympathize with management's plight with multi- million dollar salaries and bonuses—as opposed to the 55 year old who gets fired or laid off after working for the company all his/her life only to be let go without a pension or severance. Yes, managers are mean, not even efficient, and overpaid. Not every job is worth a minimum wage and many unskilled laborers can't generate that much output. The Congress that created the minimum wage knew this back in 1938, and allowed exemptions for those whose earning or productive capacity is impaired by age, physical or mental deficiency, or injury, at wages which are lower than the minimum wage. However, some workers are also overpaid, lazy, talk too much on the phone, do poor work and receive far too much pension —mine was 10%. There seems to be a trade-off between productivity and happiness.

All but the truly evil agree that if you are willing to work or are working, you shouldn't be poor. Since the rich and powerful don't seem to see that, I guess they must be truly evil.

One thing's for sure, the law of supply and demand is being toyed with and used as an excuse by management to restrict wages. Management never considers taking some of the wealth from the executives to pay higher wages. If that is done there will not have to be any price increase. What about the huge increases in pay for the executives? Didn't that enter into a price increase discussion?

The studies commissioned by the rich and powerful suggest that the long-run effects of the minimum wage are even more pronounced. These studies insinuate that over longer periods of time, businesses have an opportunity to substitute away from labor toward capital-intensive modes of production. Labor-saving capital investment becomes more attractive when low-skilled workers are made more expensive by minimum wage laws. They have been doing that for decades and that is part of the unemployment problem, and besides, they will do it anyway.

People who argue against a minimum wage usually end up making the opposition's case by saying things like, "Competition for low-wage jobs increases although high-paid jobs are unaffected." So, if unaffected, why are you bitching? Have another bonbon.

"Since a minimum wage law does not create any new resources, it does not create new jobs." (Widmaier, 2013) Don't really understand that one either. By that account then, no job exists for real estate agents, insurance salesmen, and car salesmen since they don't create any resources. There is actually some merit for that line of logic, just not in this book. Widmaier also said, "All a minimum wage law does is to prohibit employment relationships that offer wages within a certain proscribed range." I guess that means if you want too much money I will not hire you. In some rare cases, you may even be legitimately worth less as in an uneducated farm worker.

Decisions that arise for the employer would be whether to raise the wage for existing workers or get rid of them. Fortunately, the latter is costly, and there is also a certain degree of inertia in employment relations, so there may be a happy ending in the form of higher wages for some existing employees.

For those seeking the job, life may be tougher. The employer may be clever enough to attempt determination of your productivity level and if he thinks you don't muster up, he may elect to go another way.

The Bureau of Labor Statistics would have you believe that every time the minimum wage goes up, more unemployment follows. These are the people who meddle with Cost of Living increases, inflation calculations and anything else they can lie about. They would have you believe business is forced to farm out jobs offshore—whether they wanted to or not—and are forced to look for ways to automate low- or unskilled jobs. Whether they wanted to or not? It makes them sound like such nice people. These guys would sell their mothers for a nickel. Those who would eliminate minimum wages tell us that the minimum wage will cause unemployment because it prohibits some employment relationships that would otherwise have been mutually beneficial to employer and employee. Somehow I guess that means an employer believes it to be mutually beneficial if you are forced to accept paltry sub-standard wages because you are starving and have no bargaining power. Yeah, there's got to be more to it than that. So much for the level playing field. What is your option without the workers to do the work? This is beginning to sound like a game of "Blink.

How about that Technology? According to proponents of starving out society, higher minimum wages give retailers a greater incentive to automate unskilled tasks. How many of us now find the self-checkout at Home Depot or the grocery store faster and easier? One retail clerk can look over five to six customers checking out and assist them as needed. Machines don't call in sick, sue for harassment, require health insurance, or show up late. Now patrons pour their own drinks. Shoppers scan their own groceries and pump their own gas. Soon we'll be ordering from electronic tablets at our tables in sit-down restaurants to cut down on wait staff, and the cooks will be replaced by automated burger makers. (French, Minimum Wage, Maximum Stupidity, 2014)

Places like McDonald's, other fast food vendors, airports, and others have installed computer kiosks to replace workers. The flaw in the logic is that they would do that regardless of the wage rate, and have been for decades. The improvement in technology is an entirely different issue, generally again focusing on that fact that it was supposed to make life and jobs easier for workers, when all it did was put more money in the pockets of upper management. Maybe you think this is somehow for our benefit rather than that of the business. Remember when they used to wash your windshield and check your oil?

"You cannot make a man worth a given amount by making it illegal for anyone to offer him anything less. You merely deprive him of the right to earn the amount that his abilities and situation would permit him to earn, while you deprive the community even of the moderate services that he is capable of rendering." (Hazlitt, 1946) That sounds logical and might be a true statement, but the question is whether it applies to minimum wage?

The minimum wage should be the easiest issue to understand for the economically savvy. If the government arbitrarily sets a floor for wages above that set by the market, jobs will be lost. Even the Congressional Budget Office admits that 500,000 jobs would be lost with a $10.10 federal minimum wage. Who knows how high the real number would be? (French, Minimum Wage, Maximum Stupidity, 2014)

Yet here we go again with the "Raise the minimum wage" talk at a time when unemployment is still devastating much of the country. The number of Americans jobless for 27 weeks or more is still 3.37 million. And while that's only half the 6.8 million that were long-term unemployed in 2010, most of the other half didn't find work. Four-fifths of them just gave up. (French, Minimum Wage, Maximum Stupidity) If this a justification for a lower or no minimum wage, I fail to connect the dots. It seems more like a slam against the government for not providing a decent job environment.

So, good economics and better sense would say make employment cheaper? No, good economic sense would say to quit paying all the money to the CEOs. More of anything is demanded if the price goes down. That would mean lowering the minimum wage and undoing a number of cumbersome employment regulations that drive up the cost of jobs.

French goes on to say, illegal immigrants drive down wages which allows employers to invest in other things. More efficient production lowers costs for everyone, producers and consumers, allowing for capital creation. In the long run, it is capital investment that creates jobs. (French, Minimum Wage, Maximum Stupidity, 2014) Where does he get this dribble? Every statement is correct right up to the point when the greedy top management takes the money as bonuses rather than invest it in capital creation. I can only surmise that he gets his economic philosophy from some revival meeting. I prefer getting my knowledge from George Carlin and Bill Maher.

Widmaier said "minimum wage laws operate to reduce labor demand for low-skilled workers, along with the employment opportunities for low-skilled people. " (Widmaier, 2013) Who in the world ever gave him that idea? Minimum wage exists to prevent lower income people from starving. Then he said, "At the root of confusion over minimum wage laws is the false view that employers can arbitrarily pay workers whatever they want, without any economic incentives constraining this choice." With millions of people needing work, of course they can do just that. The study continued, "This attitude is exhibited in the views of people who imagine that present working conditions in industrialized economies are the result of union bargaining, rather than increases in capital and productivity." (Widmaier) Again, sheer baloney! Those who don't learn their history are doomed to repeat it. Think Industrialists of the last half of the nineteenth century. Even decent men (subject to debate), like Andrew Carnegie, didn't give a hoot about their employees unless it was to their advantage; and Carnegie was one of the best. Don't get me started on JP Morgan. Go back to 1850 and visit a factory. Do you really think working conditions would have changed if the unions had not stepped in and demanded change? Most everyone worth their salt knows about the deplorable conditions existing then and what changed it. Left to its own devices, capital and productivity improvement goes into the pockets of upper management and owners. Owners in this case not being stockholders in general.

The study concluded that such a view ignores the fact that there are laws of economics that impose themselves on employment relationships, including the laws of supply and demand. I'm guessing elasticity enters into this. Or, to be more precise, in-elasticity. If I need your product and there is no substitute for it, I will pay any price for it. One final comment. Widmaier said, "So long as labor payment of wages is an incentive to workers and a dis-utility (negative) to employers, the price of labor will be determined by supply and demand." Translated from doublespeak, what he means is employers still think of labor as a cost and not as an asset. Heaven forbid if the unions, even with all their faults, get eliminated. Management will run roughshod, and we will be back in 1850.

Whether or not a high minimum wage leads to unemployment or not is a raging issue. The unemployment rate has dropped from over 9% to around 5%. The fallacy in the numbers is regarding those who dropped off the unemployment rolls and are not counted. Four-fifths of them didn't find any work, even part time, they just gave up and dropped off the map completely.

What's worse is that the longer you are out of work, the less likely you will ever get back in. I always wonder, how *do* you give up when you need the job to eat? We could mitigate the minimum wage causes higher unemployment concern with the following argument. Pay people more when they work so they can put it away for a rainy day. Then unemployment, or retirement, doesn't hurt so much. After all, this argument works for professional athletes.

The corporate world justifies their greedy position by saying that such enormous pay packages are necessary to attract the top talent in the business world and to reward them for their efforts. What garbage. Countered and re-countered- are you telling me if we got everyone, everywhere on board, that these people wouldn't work for a paltry one million a year? Or that we couldn't do just fine substituting someone else to do the job? The people of Switzerland obviously believe that, because in 2014 they supported a referendum to give shareholders the final say on executive compensation.

The rich say higher wages should only come from production, efficiency, and capital formation—not from government decree. No doubt. The problem is when those things do improve the money/profits go to those at the top. Rent controlled units should only go to the poor, but they don't. Handicapped stickers and disability income should only go to those needing, but it doesn't. Slots at Harvard should only go to the most intelligent but check out the "quota system" and the "my Daddy donated the money for the library" system.

A perfect example of what is wrong with our system is the position held by Republican multimillionaire Ron Unz who can't seem to land on one side or the other of the debate. He starts by saying, "the minimum should be $12". Great if he had stopped there, but then he went on to say, "America doesn't want those low-paying jobs anyway. Utz continued by saying, "many of those threatened jobs are exactly the ones that should have no place in an affluent, developed society like the United States, which should not attempt to compete with Mexico or India in low-wage industries." (French, Minimum Wage, Maximum Stupidity, 2014) That's a tough argument to make and still stay politically correct. Besides, any sentence that begins with "Republican Multimillionaire" leaves a lot to be desired. Utz feels that since the fast food type jobs are here to stay and can't be shipped overseas, prices could be raised a small amount, which the poor could handle with their 40% increase in wages. Higher prices would be completely negligible to America's more affluent elements. **GREAT** His point being that if all jobs pay well enough, legal applicants will apply and take the jobs. Give him a bone on this one.

David Brat, the economics professor, although a free-market sympathizer says, "An open border is both a national security threat and an economic threat that our country cannot ignore. … Adding millions of workers to the labor market will force wages to fall and jobs to be lost" (Brat, 2014). What Brat says might be true if there were a fixed number of jobs. but, we are mostly gimmie, gimmie, so jobs are constantly created to produce the toys we want!

Mr. Unz claims that low-wage employers are being subsidized by the welfare state. "They've shifted the costs over to the taxpayer and the government," writes Unz. Instead of taxpayers supporting the poor, Unz wants business to pay. No, wait: later he writes that consumers will support the poor by paying higher prices. Utz says "McDonald's and fast-food places would probably have to raise their prices by 8 or 9 percent. Agricultural products that are American-grown would go up by less than 2 percent on the grocery shelves. And those sorts of price increases are so small that they would be almost unnoticed in most cases by the consumer." (French, Minimum Wage, Maximum Stupidity, 2014) Walmart would cover a $12 minimum wage with a one-time price increase of 1.1%, he says, with the average Walmart shopper paying just an extra $12.50 a year. So it's consumers—who are also taxpayers—who get to be the lender of last resort with Unz's plan. (French, Minimum Wage, Maximum Stupidity) Economist Ludwig von Mises thought rates were determined by expenses. The price paid for labor is included in the price of the product (von Mises, 1912) Mises also said a general rate of wages does not exist because labor is very different in quality. (von Mises) This is included here to indicate that even a relatively well thought of economist like von Moses can be wrong. Prices are not a function of expenses anymore, at least not totally. The profit added to include the high paid CEO is very arbitrary and usually quite high.

If you really want a higher paying job they say you could go to work in Alaska or in the North Dakota oil fields. But Roy Rogers movies aside, that rough and ready, gun-toting, bar-room brawling, beat your wife atmosphere isn't quite all its cut out to be. Gets old real quick. Plus, good old greed quickly eats up the extra wages through higher rents, food costs, and other basics. It's still human nature at work.

Where are we headed? What will the future bring? Wage increases do not keep up with price increases. There is no question that seniors on a fixed income don't keep up. Minimum wage increases and the accompanying price hikes disproportionately affect seniors as a group. Social Security's cost of living increases do not keep up with the cost of living. Each time minimum wages go up, they push the buying power of a fixed income down.

Because of the inequality existing in the system, seniors will be retiring more and more with insufficient means. They are living longer and will run out of money.

Part of that is their fault because they overspent and didn't save enough. People also expect to live far more comfortable lives than that to which they are entitled. Many of those "poor" seniors actually had relatively good jobs while in their prime. They just spent every bit of what they made, and then some, living the American dream. Some of those people played all of their lives and don't deserve anything, while other worked hard, lost jobs through downsizing, or were just unlucky. Those who are cautious, live within their budget and set aside their money seem to be the outsiders today. They are laughed at by the live today crowd. Sort of like they laughed at Noah for wasting his time building an Ark. The second half of the equations is that of the unfairness. Too much money is in the hands of far too few rich people. Those receiving benefits believe those funds are too meager, while those paying taxes think they're too high.

So we live in a country where an organization can afford multi-million dollar CEOs, yet $10 per hour is going to break the bank for them?

Dr. Pierce's Budget

Following are some numbers generated by Dr. Diana Pierce regarding the amounts necessary for a minimum subsistence. Her purpose was to indicate that lower income folks do not have enough money and that even programs developed for them are not adequate. Pierce looked at a number of options from: different wage levels—minimum wages, welfare leavers, $10 per hour and $12 per hour, as well as different scenarios—wages alone, with subsidies, and other options. For the purpose of simplicity, this information was condensed. Pierce says that self-sufficiency is around $10.45 per hour for each of two people working or $3,677 per month or $44,123. That figure compared against a government program nowhere near that amount and even worse, numerous individual families who cannot seem to earn anywhere near that much. Incidentally, a single adult must earn $18.35 hour to earn $3,230/month (Solman, 2013). Below is a low to medium budget as of 2009.

Housing	800
Food	500
Misc-paper etc	285- hair, nails, haircuts, soap, deodorant, toothpaste
Child care	1000
Clothes	50- Children grow!
Health care	260- How likely is this?
Utilities-Water	50
Electric/Gas	100
Transportation	210
Car repair	50
Car insurance	100
Taxes	800

House/renters ins.	30
Life Insurance	50
Phone	100
Computer	50
TV	50
Real estate taxes	80 optional
Christmas	100
Savings	200
Entertainment	110
Total	$4975
Child tax credit	-170
Child care tax credit	-100

Now you know why we are in trouble as a nation. Granted, some of these items can be eliminated but as a rough guide, this is significantly more than welfare or minimum wage. Obviously, child care jumps out at you as an item that needs to be addressed. Fortunately, it is an area that can be addressed with government help. Other than that, we need to either reduce the costs of goods, raise the wages, or redistribute the wages.

There is no tuition for educational improvement. It should be free anyway—paid by government. Even $12 per hour doesn't cover this kind of budget. Plus, this is not an extravagant budget. It needs to be understood that many benefits and the ability to make ends meet also depend on the state in which you live. As an example, the eligibility for child care in Florida is cut off at $2,500.

In Missouri it's $1,400. Big difference. These numbers do not work in expensive cities. There is further research required here regarding the Federalists versus State's rights. Various work support packages include: child care assistance, welfare to work packages (child care, food stamps, Medicaid, and housing subsidies). Pierce also states that, among our many problems, 9 of 20 of the occupations that will add the most jobs in 2012 are only averaging $19,600 (Pearce, 2012).

Child Care

A 2014 study from UNISEF found that "the United States ranks 36th out of the 41 wealthy countries included in the UNICEF report when it comes to child care. And these other countries are not all heavy hitters. We're talking about countries such as Greece, Spain and Mexico that we just barely edged out. Those who are better than we are include: Lithuania, Croatia, Romania, Turkey, Bulgaria, Hungary, Slovakia, and Cyprus. Not exactly banana republics but nothing to write home about either. No surprise that we got clobbered by the likes of Austria, Switzerland, France, Japan, Germany and England. "32.2 percent of U.S. children live in households with an income below 60 percent of the national median income – about $31,000 annually." (Ingraham, 2014) Please remember that when it comes to figures, especially from the government, "liars figure and figures lie." Who knows whether they do it on purpose or are just trying too hard to be cleaver? I say this because they used 2008 benchmark income because the income levels have fallen since then. If I think real hard I may even be able to figure that one out. "The number of children in poverty is up an additional 1.7 million children from 2008 to 2012. Of that increase in the OECD and/or EU, nearly a third are here in the United States." (Ingraham) Now it's three more years! How bad do you think it is now? Recall that things are only getting worse. There are no solutions in the wind here in good the old USA. For any of our problems.

I keep hearing blowhards tell me we are the richest country in the world. Frankly, I'd be embarrassed to say that and also have one of the world's highest childhood poverty rates as well as our high infant mortality rate. Seems like the health and well-being of our children would be paramount to us as policymakers and human beings. Disgusting. In our country today these problems only go in one direction- worse. The tie in and the problem, I speculate is the bulk of all the money is going to very few at the top that could be used to solve these issues. It will be interesting to see the results of Obama care over the years.

Following are just a few of the nations and their rightful place in the Child Poverty Hall of Fame. The percentage is the amount of children living in poverty:

Norway	6.3%
Finland	8.8%
Denmark	10.2%
Slovakia	11.1%
Sweden	12.1%
Czech Republic	12.8%
Australia	13.0%
Slovenia	13.4%
Poland	14.5%
Netherlands	13.9%
Switzerland	14.7%
Austria	14.2%
Germany	15.0%
Korea	16.8%
France	18.6%
Japan	19.0%
Canada	20.8%
Portugal	23.6%
United Kingdom	25.6%
Ireland	28.6%
Italy	30.3%
United States	32.2%
Mexico	34.0%
Spain	36%
Israel	36%

Those espousing elimination a minimum wage say having it prevents wages from floating when needed within the capitalistic economy. They say those earning above the minimum wages will then want increases also. Probably true enough. Although I acknowledged greed knows no class distinction, so what? How come that issue doesn't apply to CEO pay? Why can't it be reduced when times are tough?

Social Security

Why would people with so much money and power begrudge other a pittance? Social Security is one of those bewildering examples. The Republicans have been trying to kill this program for years. Is it because it is popular and, in spite of everything the rich say, working pretty well? What's not to like if it provides a small morsel for the elderly to help in their golden years? Or is it just because these people have no clue what's happening in the lower ranks? The rich do lead such sheltered lives that they really wonder, "Have they no cake?" The wealthy and powerful don't seem to realize that many people on social security work manual labor jobs so their life expectancy hasn't gone up. Plus their salaries haven't gone up and there is no longer a pension plan in place for them. Stephen Moore, a right wing activist, calls it "the soft underbelly of the welfare state" (Krugman, 2015)

During his tenure as Commander of Nothing Bush wanted to privatize Social Security. I believe if the average person had been capable of handling their own finances we would have done that way back before Social security was enacted. It's a security blanket and therefore should not be gambled with. Unfortunately many of us are gamblers and need a little help and guidance.

I suspect that raising the retirement age another year is like stepping over a dollar to pick up a dime. Come on guys, you can do better than that. Job Bush (no matter how hard I try, I can't stop seeing his brother in him) says that "the retirement age should be pushed back to 68 or 70. Scott Walker agrees. Marco Rubin wants both to raise the retirement age and to cut benefits for higher-income seniors. Even Rand Paul wants to raise the retirement age to 70 and means-test benefits. That should be fun to administer. Ted Cruz wants to revive the Bush privatization plan." (Krugman, 2015) That should be reason enough to vote Democrat. You would think that since Americans love social security the Republicans would at least pretend to want to help.

The question to ponder is why do the rich hate Social Security so much? They don't even pay into it to the full extent of their earnings, there's a cap on social security.

CHAPTER EIGHT - YOU HAVE TO LAUGH

Sports Jokes

We joke all the time about dumb football players—yet they are paid a king's ransom. The rationale being because they can only play for a dozen years or so they have to make hay while the sun shines is sheer crap. It's the same theory given by carpenters, etc., due to bad weather. Wow! I bet lots of folks would love to be paid double the amount to work half the time. What screwed up logic! I can't tell if the people advancing the theory are stupid or they think everyone else is.

To cement the fact that we may be paying the wrong people outrageous sums of money, here are a few tidbits illustrating the point:

Ohio State's Urban Meyer joked once about one of his players, "He doesn't know the meaning of the word fear. In fact, I just saw his grades, and he doesn't know the meaning of a lot of words."

Why do Tennessee fans wear orange? So they can dress that way for the game on Saturday, go hunting on Sunday, and pick up trash on Monday.

How many Michigan freshmen football players does it take to change a light bulb? None. That's a sophomore course.

A University of Cincinnati football player was almost killed yesterday in a tragic horseback-riding accident. He fell from a horse and was nearly trampled to death. Luckily, the manager of the Walmart came out and unplugged the horse.

What do you say to a University of Miami Hurricane football player dressed in a three-piece suit?" "Will the defendant please rise."

If three Florida State football players are in the same car, who is driving? The police officer.

University of Michigan Coach Brady Hoke is only going to dress half of his players for the game this week; the other half will have to dress themselves.

I don't know who came up with those but they're on the money. Why don't we just cap all of their pay at a maximum of $300,000 for athletes, musicians, actors, and CEO. No loopholes.

AIG- also a joke

Speaking of unfair bailouts and a twisted sense of right and wrong; have you heard the AIG line? First, they whined that the execs were entitled to their bonuses by contracts made before the feds put in any money. The company couldn't unilaterally break its contracts. Second, the firm needed to maintain the quality of its management. Especially, now that it is owned by the government, it needs good people to make sure the taxpayers get a good return on their investments. Does anybody believe a word these people say anymore? The answer to the first argument is, who cares? The answer to the second one is, given the quality of the top management at AIG and the mess they created, bad management would be a step up.

If this isn't enough to make you cry, let me stir the pot. "Hank Greenberg, an investor in AIG, and former CEO, is now suing the government because he says AIG didn't need the government and could have gotten along just fine without the bailout. He thinks the government somehow cheated the shareholders." (Smith Y. , 2013) I guess he didn't read the fine print for bankruptcies, which says shareholders usually end up with nothing. Funny he didn't say anything at the time. These guys have some gall. We should all put this one in our management playbook.

I once read where the AIG bonuses were a Humiliation for Wall Street. What in the world ever made that person think amoral people with no conscience can be humiliated?

An anonymous source once expressed how remarkable it is that the public has an opinion about how much insurance executives should be paid. You're damn right we have an opinion! Our insurance premiums pay the jerks' salary.

Edward Liddy returned to head up AIG during the government bailout. He said the non-payment of agreed upon bonuses to employees would be a terrible thing. Why? The bonuses didn't even accomplish their stated goal—to retain employees. Andrew Cuomo,

New York's attorney general, said that 52 employees who received bonuses had since left AIG. So much for that plan. Why is the honor always one sided?

The problem is, nothing Liddy says has a ring of impartiality to it. He is one of them. He is part of the broken executive pay system. As the chairman of Allstate from 1999 to 2007, when the company's stock under-performed those of its rivals, he made $137 million (Bonner, 2009). They called part of his reward, "A tool for retaining executive talent." Another load of crap. Sort of like Hank Paulson as Treasury Secretary protecting the government from his old pals on Wall Street. Who do you know who can stand that kind of temptation? Do you really think Liddy was objective about retention bonuses?

As to the difficulty of replacing those AIG employees, please. Maybe a slight few might have a better handle on the toxic portfolio they helped build. They should take a lesson from their own playbook, or that of any large corporation. Give the guy 10 minutes notice to clear out his desk and escort him to the door. His remaining behind will only make others toxic. The bonuses averaged $395,000 for over 400 employees. Indispensable? Give me a break.

Twinkie Defense and other Fun Stuff

Ever heard of the Twinkie defense? Not to worry. Just the most ridiculous twisting of legal logic and human nature ever perpetrated. In 1979, Dan White, a sorry loser of a county supervisor in San Francisco got a gun, carried it into City Hall, shooting and killing Harvey Milk and George Moscone. His lawyer said he was high on sugar (Twinkies). He got five years for a double premeditated murder. Yet there are people in jail for 20 years for a Marijuana charge.

Did you follow the Hostess bankruptcy? In this case: "the devil made me do it", unions being the devil. What a load of bull! One article termed it shameless and delusional. Great phrases. It could apply to most of what goes on in the world of the rich and famous.

Management always says the unions must accept pay and benefit cuts to "save the company." It should sound familiar because that's exactly the same thing that happened the last time the company went into bankruptcy. Always ask for pay concessions from workers. With Hostess, they got them in 2004. This time the unions said shove it. Rightly so.

Have you ever noticed that the spin doctors and gullible press often seem to blame the troubles on labor costs? Granted the press will leap on almost anything for a story so no surprise here.

Hostess Brands is the perfect example of private equity vultures and executives paying themselves outrageous bonuses from a viable company, loading it up with debt, and then blaming the problems of cash shortages that then occurred on labor and wanting them to make up the difference. During the 1960s and 70s the original company went on a spending spree. It also went private, then public again (Hiltzik, Poor management, not union intransigence, killed Hostess, 2012). Do you think this had anything to do with the fees the middlemen and insiders received?

Each time Hostess bought something they did it with a lot of debt, usually called junk bonds. Although that debt is obtained with the security of the income stream and assets of the company being bought, there's a reason the bonds are called junk. My guess is there is never enough income or assets to warrant the amount of debt issued. So, the next item in the playbook is to declare bankruptcy to reduce the debt just incurred. At the same time we have to get rid of a lot of workers, because it's their fault we're bloated. Then we can go out and load up with more debt. I'll bet you think the CEO at the time wasn't paid millions. Just before the second bankruptcy Hostess tripled the CEO's compensation (Hiltzik, Poor management, not union intransigence, killed Hostess,

2012). You couldn't make this stuff up. Where do I sign?

Now I'm not saying the unions are without fault. Remember, human nature rules. Way back in the late 1800s and early 1900s there was surely a need for someone to protect the worker. Upper management was running wild while conditions were deplorable and wages languished. Forget about benefits; get sick and you die. But somewhere along the line the unions became organized crime. Even if not illegal they were pulling the same crap that management was. This manifested itself glaringly in the automotive industry. Although I believe everyone should have a roof over their head, having a Rolls Royce in the garage isn't what I had in mind. No doubt everyone in the automotive industry was guilty, management and labor. Besides, now you have three players—management, union workers, and those not in a union. That inequality meant those without union representation were really left behind. The union worker became just another privileged minority out of touch with the average person. It doesn't take long for those rising up to become just like the masters. Think Orwell's *Animal Farm* or the French Revolution. In the case of the U.S. union worker, he became lazy and stopped working hard.

Maybe if we as a nation took the money from the rich instead of the middle class, the Affordable

Care Act and other good programs would not get such bad press.

Clearly too many people are getting benefits they haven't earned. Just one more task ahead.

Thank God Mitt Romney didn't win the presidency. He would have been the poster boy for this debased era of American capitalism, having made his money at Bain Capital in just this manner. I don't know how, but the American people actually got it right that time. I guess if you bet red all the time it will eventually come up.

One solution to inequality in general, and certainly for companies like Hostess would be a reform of the loopholes that allow the pillagers to take huge tax deductions for loading up a company with debt in order to take it over (many times only to break it up and destroy jobs) and then pay themselves exorbitant dividends that further strip the operating company of resources. Another would be to send some of these guys to prison, and I don't mean country club prisons. I have to ask for the umpteenth time, is it ever going to end? Is life just structured for the haves? No, seriously, I want to know so I can just retire if there is really no hope.

CHAPTER NINE - HOPE ON THE HORIZON

Thomas Piketty

"Thomas Piketty mocks the economics profession for its "childish passion for mathematics. But that doesn't mean he doesn't back up his assertions with facts. (Krugman, 2014) Big difference between facts and subjective interpretations with graphs.

Piketty feels that not only does the United States have a much more unequal income distribution but that it is mainly the governments fault that it exists. (Krugman, 2014). Even though the Europeans are hot on our heels in regards to income inequality, though still left behind in our dust, they then make up for the practice somewhat by way of taxation. This illustrates that it is human nature to be greedy but that there are still varying degrees to it, and some control can be exerted over the greed with measurable results. Not only do the Europeans demonstrate that taxation works (in spite of what screaming you may hear in the newspaper from French movie stars) but it should be progressive. A flat tax would not address the huge gap in raw income. Remember, the 75% tax in France is only on an amount over and above several hundred thousand euros.   Piketty feels that capital should be counted when measuring the inequality gap, unlike most modern economists, who rely on ordinary income. His reasoning is that at the top of the income ladder, capital gains are more predominate, just like his

Belle Epoque period one hundred years ago.. No matter what is said to the contrary, once you have it, you have to work really hard to lose it.

Economic growth and income inequality are tied together. Most modern economists agree that as growth decreases, so does the return from capital. Piketty says that may be true but it doesn't decrease as much. If he is correct, and he appears to be, then in a slow growth environment such as we have had for around 40 years, the gap widens. Yep, sure seems like. For example, assume a 1-2% growth rate in the economy and a 4-5% capital growth rate, which is exactly what's happening and what did happen one hundred years ago. (Krugman, 2014) Technical advances allowing management to replace workers with machines exacerbates this phenomena. The technical term for this is the elasticity of substitution. (Krugman)

Those benefiting from the phenomena (rich people, capitalists, bankers, corporate CEOs etc say that is not the case. Of course they would say that, wouldn't they? History tells another story, otherwise the gap wouldn't exists, right? This redistribution comes in the form of corporate profits, dividends, rents, sales of property, and increase in property values. Take the blinders off and read the news. Corporate profits are up, therefore dividends are up, rents and real estate prices are up.

Thomas Piketty is French, so he has a few things going for him over the average American. He is a lot classier. Maybe not such a big deal except for the time worn saying that "those who fail to read their history are doomed to repeat it." Because of this Piketty has a better working knowledge of the "Belle Epoque" period and before in Europe. Krugman references Piketty's story of Balzac's Pere Goriot, but most American would be more familiar, and therefore comfortable, with Jane Austin's *Pride and Prejudice*, having probably seen it on television. The gist of both stories as well as that of many writers in that era is the importance of inherited wealth. The illustration given by Piketty was from Goriot but it's the same tired cliché; it's better to marry rich than to try to get rich by working, even if you finally do make it big. During that infamous time the richest one percent controlled 60 percent of the wealth in France and 70 percent in Britain. In France in 2015 it's back to 70% and rising. (Krugman, 2014)

There is one major difference between now and one hundred years ago; today, on top of the inheritance inequity builder, high compensation is making the numbers way beyond ludicrous. In addition to the infamous "Rise of the Machines", we can now add the "Rise of the Supersalaries." (Krugman, 2014) "Real wages for most US workers have increased little if at all since the early 1970s, but wages for the top one percent of earners have risen 165 percent, and wages for the top 0.1 percent have risen 362 percent. If Balzac's Rastignac were alive today, Vautrin might concede that he could in fact do as well by becoming a hedge fund manager as he could by marrying wealth." (Krugman)

Donald Trump

A favorite example of this is the current political baboon flavor of the month, Donald Trump. Sure, many people squander the inheritance they are given. More the pity for them. They can be criticized. But those on the other end who increase the family fortune do not get any credit or accolades. Inflation alone would account for a significant increase in wealth. Top management and talent make 10 times what they made 30 years ago, let alone 100 years ago when comparing what someone inherited. So Trump's $35 million inheritance would be worth a few billion dollars (a factor of ten in 30 years and a factor again of ten for the next twenty or thirty years) on inflation alone after 50 years since Daddy left him a fortune. That doesn't even begin to take into account the contacts his father left him. Once you are in the game (it's who you know), it is hard not to make money. You have unlimited funds to borrow, insider information, cheap labor for your various endeavors and a lax system that's allows you extra time to get it right. Then when you can't make money in spite of all the advantages and get in trouble, you use the tools of business, such as bankruptcy to basically renege on your obligations at the expense of whomever you are forcing to take less on the debt you owe them.

Then there's the personality. Everything I stand for is against aggression, which unfortunately is a way of life here in the United States. We, and many others, have taken Survival of the Fittest to a level it was never intended to be. Trump exemplifies that. He is mean, prejudiced, looks down on people, makes fun of people's personal traits, and can't control his big mouth. There is also a chance that he doesn't believe a word he is spouting, just politically doing what his advisers say is the right thing to say. Come to think of it, those are exactly the qualifications for a great President.

Superstars

The proponents who justify this income inequality refer to the justification espoused in the 1981 paper titled *The Economics of Superstars,* written by economist Sherwin Rosen, who argued that "modern communications technology, by extending the reach of talented individuals, was creating winner-take-all markets in which a handful of exceptional individuals reap huge rewards, even if they're only modestly better at what they do than far less well paid rivals." (Krugman, 2014) Notice that he ends by saying these Superstars are only modestly better? Then why should they not be paid just modestly more? Again, the expression "winner take all" leaves a sour taste in my mouth. No question that hard work should be rewarded. Capitalism came from the protestant work ethic I suppose. That's an admirable work ethic, but can it go too far? Probably, as in all things, a little is good, a lot becomes onerous. Besides, who exactly is doing all the hard work? It would also appear to be very hard to assess just what portion of responsibility and therefore credit should be given to the CEO. How in the world do you know if the profits a company makes is due to efficient workers, luck, right place/right time, or simply inflation in the numbers? You got to love the last one. The government forces the value of all assets and prices up and then the CEOs take credit for that artificial increase as having hit their numbers and therefore, having earned their bonus. This thing about CEOs making so much because they are worth it and create such wonderful things just isn't true. The creative, innovative work- medical breakthroughs, computers (Steve Jobs was not the genius behind the technology), iPhones (of dubious real use), etc are done by some lab rat making $80,000 per year. All the

CEO does is shuffle money, and even then not with the right or most useful intent.

Unfortunately, that's not an issue in the ivory towers of the corporate offices. Compensation is determined by a committee, usually appointed by the CEO himself, or by a board filled with your cronies. So you set your own pay, based on social and political norms and not economics. The fear is that, "say it enough and it becomes fact." The longer the rich are allowed to get away with this travesty, the more ingrained it will become and pretty soon it will seem acceptable, even to those who are starving. Piketty opines that tax could play a part in this aw well. When the top tax rate is very high, there is little incentive, even for the corrupt, to push the envelope. But when they and their buddies get the tax rate nice and low, then they have real incentive. (Krugman, 2014)

Piketty and Krugman both agree that there are many factors that affect economics, including population growth and technological improvements. But the bottom line is that, as Scrooge said, things can be changed- by the political community. The will to do something good is very weak, however, history doesn't paint a picture of any great hope. Even as a result of the French Revolution, those who came to power soon become the tyrants. As Upton Sinclair famously declared, "it is difficult to get a man to understand something when his salary depends on his not understanding it." Piketty came up with his own similar justification. "No hypocrisy is too great when economic and financial elites are obliged to defend their interest." (Krugman, 2014)

The study by Thomas Piketty and Emmanuel Saez determined that 95 percent of the gains from economic recovery since 2009 have gone to the top 1 percent. In fact, more than 60 percent of the gains went to the top 0.1 percent, people with annual incomes of more than $1.9 million. (Krugman, 2013)

Paul Krugman

"There are, it turns out, people in the corporate world who will do whatever it takes, including fraud that kills people, in order to make a buck. We need effective regulation to police that kind of bad behavior." (Krugman, 2015) You would think the good guys in corporate should want some regulation; it would help to level the playing field for them when competing with the truly unscrupulous. (Krugman)

Want to know just what kind of a culture we have here in the United States? Turing Pharmaceuticals doesn't do any life altering drug development. They merely buy existing drugs and jack up the prices, like from $13.50 a tablet to $750. (Krugman, 2015) I doubt they are the only ones. What a business plan- and so helpful for the overall economy and quality of life. You can bet the CEO is doing OK though. Actually this is just too illustrative of our corruption to stop there. When caught with his pants down, the CEO of Turing promised to reduce the price. Of course, he didn't say when or to what price. And he says it is necessary for them to fund research. Blah, Blah, Blah. This guy is typical of everything that's wrong in this country, and perhaps world. No doubt the guy is very smart; however, that is totally offset by his blatant arrogance, his willingness to tread right on the line between right and wrong, and giving people the finger (see, just a child) on his Twitter account. He was fired by a previous company for poor management skills including his outspoken use of Twitter. A brash, relatively young, hedge fund type who would say and do anything for a nickel. His picture sitting with a chess board is actually a little scary. A mini Donald Trump, in other words. Is it OK to think and speak badly of someone who jacks up a price from $13 to $750? In Britain, GlaxoSmithKline sells the drug for 66 cents a pill, and in India, it costs even less, so you be the judge. Welcome to America.

"Too many important players now argue, in effect, that business can do no wrong and that government has no role to play in limiting misbehavior." (Krugman, 2015) There is no doubt that our government is horrible in many ways, but they truly seem to be outgunned here by big business.

History says that if you trust corporations and individuals to do the right thing, they won't

CHAPTER TEN - OUT OF CONTROL

The Rich Get Richer

It would appear it doesn't take any special brains to become rich either. Figure where the wealth came from: 20% are just mean and pushy, 20% just got lucky—in the right place at the right time, 15% inherited it, 15% are some kind of overpaid "talent" who can't spell cat, or would kill one if they could, 15% are undeservingly on disability, leaving 15% who are decent humans and worked really hard.

Do you really think there are people out there who are better than you? Well, if you don't, then how can you put up with this CEO business? Even when they get fired for doing a lousy job they get millions in severance. I want to puke!

The other side (those in favor of income inequality and favoritism) would have you believe not only do they earn and deserve the money but also they spend their days whining about how you even found out how much they were making. Investors see these high compensations and wonder why the higher ups are getting paid so much when the company is not doing well. This deluded group of either ill-informed motor mouths or wanna be rich people themselves go on to say, "CEOs are like heart surgeons that make critical decisions on a daily basis. They paint a picture of a poor put-upon, harried individual swamped by volatile markets, gripping shareholders wanting better returns so why would anyone even want the job? They continue, "CEOs cannot relax on their laurels because it's never good enough. They have to be well-informed in a changing world. They have to be experts in time management, prioritization, and delegation. Gee, don't we also, in our jobs or as parents? All this for a measly $10,000,000 per year. I believe I need the services of one of those heart surgeons. After reading this dribble I realize why people can't see eye to eye. Whoever wrote this had to be in someone's pocket. I never heard such slop. The tear jerkers go on to say that family life can be strained. Whose fault is that? Besides, life ain't so great in the ghetto either. The writer even went so far as to call these people phenomenal and rare individuals. Seriously, phenomenal? You better take another look at this spectacle of a man/woman. I'm thinking we have our priorities in the wrong place. Either that or the writer has a crush on one of these guys.

Not done yet, the soap opera continues, saying there are not enough of these wonderful specimens so the companies get into bidding wars because otherwise they will lose out and the CEO will go to the competition. This also increases the pay rate. Do you hear yourself? I think the pay is outrageous because those making the decisions are board members with an agenda. What's good for the goose is good for the gander and the time will roll around when they will be up for more pay at their own company, with that same CEO on their board. Or the guy is merely your drinking buddy.

Really, if the job is that tough, then back off and enjoy life more. Concentrate on making the world a nicer place to live. Or give the job to someone else.

By the way, just like the threat that the rich will run away if taxed too much, if they are going to be hired for more by someone else, get together with that someone else and strike a deal. Collude. That's what the CEOs would do. Since it's so easy for you and you're so much smarter than the rest of us, why not redistribute, and we'll let *you* start over again? You keep saying how you will have it all back again quickly.

Do you realize it only took five years or less for the greedy CEOs to get back on the horse and start taking bonuses again? A few years back, much was made of those same guys deciding not to take a bonus. It just goes to show you one year does not a trend make. You can bet they got a lot of mileage out of that nonsense. So how much credit do you get for "only" taking $600,000 when you got $68 million the previous year?

"Between 45 and 50 million people live below the poverty line of $23,283, meaning a family of four with two adults and two children. That's 25% of the population. The bottom 20% of the US population saw its real household income peak in 1999 at $13,663 (in 2012 dollars). Thirteen years later, it had lost 16% of its wealth, with real household income of only $11,490." (Gongloff, 2014) Most people would be lucky to get $20–30 per hour, especially the young recent graduates up through their mid-thirties. So, say $30 per hour for an additional 25% of the population (that's around $60,000). Average person makes $50,000 per year. Most college professors (no matter what your biased opinion of them is, they are smart and well-educated), are lucky to make between $60,000 and $80,000 per year.

It is painfully evident to me that in the developed world workers have failed to benefit from the uneven global economic recovery.

"From 2002 through 2010, Goldman, Morgan Stanley, Merrill Lynch, Lehman, and Bear Stearns paid out $312 billion in compensation and benefits to their employees." (Grey, 2008) That is more than the budget for most of the countries in the world. In my opinion, certainly the collapse of Lehman Brothers and Bear Stearns was due in part to being leveraged by over 30-to-1! That means a 3% move against you and you are under water without equity. This fact in no way takes away from the outrageous compensation given to the CEOs and other top management on Wall Street. Plus, whether you have any sympathy or not for the shareholders, these were public companies that were supposed to have a duty to these shareholders. Now I believe that employees are extremely important as stakeholders also but, how does handing out $312 billion in compensation and bonuses to your employees add value to a public company? Besides, why not hire some more people and spread the wealth around? I would say that the money should be distributed more evenly also, except I just remembered the above-mentioned secretary who received $622,000. This must be the only industry where the "little guy" gets some of the pie. Don't kid yourself though, in thinking that most of the wealth didn't go to those at the top. Can you say, "Out of control?" These shenanigans during a time when their industry received the $700 billion bailout as a reward for causing the trouble in the first place. Millions of people have asked why some form of tie in to compensation should have been instituted for any company receiving bailout money. The tie in philosophy should be applied to every corporation. Make all compensation, or at least bonuses and stock options tie to layoffs, a percentage of average employee pay, profits, stock price, and do it over a 5- or 10-year period—even if the guy leaves the company. Since it didn't happen I guess that tells you what those in the control group think of you and me. All because Wall Street destroyed the system.

You have to laugh when honest people actually think the guy across the desk selling you stocks is your friend or has your interests at heart. This creep is a peddler and will say whatever it takes to earn a commission. At the higher levels on Wall Street, greed and corruption run so rampant it makes you dizzy. Insider information, cronyism, and just plain lies. We need to put someone in prison, and not a country club minimum security one either. Let's face it, incarceration is a deterrent.

It's important to note that the richies say the sums they are being paid would not have saved the economy. Maybe, but it would send a message of decency. Besides, every little bit helps, and I have a feeling it might do more than you think. Add in all the obscene sport's figures', movie stars' and musicians' pay, and I'll bet it would help a lot.

Everything is relative, of course, so when you hear bonuses have plunged by fifty percent, that means they are now just ridiculous. How many times do you have to be slapped in the face with numbers? Wall Street personnel make millions in a year. Some of us make $50,000. Managing directors in investment banking are expected to get average bonuses of $1 million in 2008, the WSJ says. In commodities, the same level executives are looking at a 25% drop in the average bonus—to $3.5 million to $4 million. And you know where that bonus money came from, right? Yep, bailout money from the government. Some of these schmucks should be grateful to have a job. When, by the way, did bonuses become automatic? That's not what the word means.

CEOs of the top 50 largest corporations average about $15 million, regardless of whether or not the company makes any profit. KB Homes, for example, lost $929 million in 2007, its share price fell 70%. Still, CEO Mezger got paid 1,000 times more than the average employee. (Kristoff, 2009)

"Professors at Harvard and Cornell found that CEO pay at companies in the Standard & Poor's 500 index rose almost three times over 10 years, to an average of $10.3 million in 2002. Between 1998 and 2002, executive pay accounted for 10 percent of total corporate profit. By 2006 executive pay was at 66%. Goldman Sachs, Merrill Lynch, Bear Stearns, Lehman Brothers, and Morgan Stanley bonuses totaled $60 billion in 2006—double the year's earnings of the five firms." (Bonner & Rajiva, 2007) And the largest bonuses are certainly skewed toward the top few.

If you had put $10,000 into the stocks of companies with the highest-paid CEOs of the previous year from January 1991 to December 2004, you would have ended up with only $8,079, while the same money invested in the S&P 500 would have returned you $48,350—that is, six times as much. (Bonner, 2007b)

Inflation Favors the Rich

Without the requirement for backing by gold after 1971 there was an explosion of credit. Credit is handled by the credit industry (banking and Wall Street), so they found themselves in a favorable position. The middle and lower classes lose out because they went in debt to buy things. The rich, who owned stocks and bonds, got richer. Profits in the financial industry quadrupled from 1970 to 2007. Salaries in the financial industry also increased dramatically.

As most institutions mature, they gradually shift from existing to serve their constituents, to manipulation by and self-preservation of those who control it. It becomes entrenched and resists any change that would diminish the power and wealth of the controlling groups. It becomes very parasitic and drains resources away from production.

The rich have most of the stock that benefits from inflation. They own most of the real estate, with the exception of the house most of us live in.

Tying the two together, those rich people who own all the apartments, offices, and shopping centers have mortgages on them so the real cost of those mortgages goes down while the value goes up.

Why is it that every time a government boondoggle is put in place the rich get richer? Think about TSA (which probably doesn't even work), the wars in Iraq and Afghanistan (where we are not wanted except to protect them and then go away), stimulus projects (which goes to the banks and no farther), sadly the running of health care and many others (chalked up to the greed and incompetence of human nature). Let's face it, insiders are usually smart, definitely well-connected, and generally amoral shysters. That's a tough combination to beat. It seems as though the farther down the road, as societies go from producers to moochers, the spread between the rich and the rest of us becomes greater.

Central banks lend to "too big to fail" insider banks and their buddies at rates below inflation. And yet, even with the ridiculously cheap money, bankers still manage to lose money, after paying big bonuses, of course. Besides, if and when they get in trouble and go broke, the Fed will be there to bail them out. How can you lose money when all you are doing is giving the money right back to the government without any risk? Even if you don't go broke that is hardly a management plan to be rewarded with bonuses. A monkey could do that. Sometimes these bankers actually work against the Fed's game plan, first by not lending to business ventures and secondly by speculating and driving up asset prices. Well, I guess the asset bubbles are what the government wants, come to think about it, but higher food and energy prices sure don't help the average worker. None of this provides any worthwhile job, mind you.

There is an insidious misconception here about inflation—not that it has a huge bearing on CEO pay. However, it bears repeating. It's like the housing market. If you didn't have a house to begin with, you don't get a chance to participate in the inflation! You have to be on the treadmill or you get left behind. It is an asset and CEOs have more assets so keep doing better and better.

"These people are wrong on moral grounds and wrong on policy grounds," says Steven Rattner, who currently oversees former NYC Mayor Michael Bloomberg's investments as chairman of Willett Advisors LLC. "On a practical level, if the people in the 1% don't recognize the 99% are hurting, they're going to end up with far more severe consequences then if they were simply willing to do something now. Those consequences could include civil unrest and "more punitive legislation," such as much higher tax rates for the wealthiest, he says. On a moral level, the whining of the 1% is particularly appalling, Rattner continues, noting overall median incomes have fallen about 7% in the past 12 years on an inflation-adjusted basis and by 25% since 1979 for the average American without a high school diploma." (Task, 2014)

What kind of logic says that when you are losing your shirt you hire a new CEO and pay him/her millions right up front? Is there no one in your existing organization qualified to take the reins? If not, then shame on you, you really do have a crummy organization and should be allowed to fail.

All of today's benefits are going to a limited group (corporations and their corporate officers) and not being equally distributed among other members of the workforce. CEOs in the United States are way too expensive. American companies are busily outsourcing workers when they should be in-sourcing CEOs from other countries.

Consulting after Retirement

Wouldn't you think that retiring CEOs would be willing to consult for free after they retire? After all, the company made them millionaires? The companies use the excuse that they need to continue paying these guys otherwise they will go to work for a competitor. I thought that's what non-compete agreements were for? Most of these retirees get more money for less time spent and every perk known to man. Think jet planes, offices, cars, expenses, computers, phones etc. The really neat thing is when these vultures become consultants the corporations don't even have to make a profit. They get paid regardless. Nice work if you can get it.

Do they still give out gold watches for the guy who worked 40 years in the mail-room?

"Ex-Source Interlink Cos. Chairman and CEO S. Leslie Flegel landed a 41% pay raise for his part-time consulting job with the company. He receives $1 million a year in the three-year consulting gig, which could also reward him with up to $4 million in bonus pay. That's compared to his 2005 salary and bonus of $710,683. He also received a $4.7 million severance package and a $900,000 bonus. This from a company that sells and distributes DVDs, CDs, magazines, and books" (Brush, 2006). No war monger, no Wall Street firm, no advanced medical bio-tech firm.

"Joseph Luter III was chief executive at Smithfield Foods. Stock options and grants helped him get 4.7 million shares worth $127 million. In his last three years he collected $20.2 million in bonuses and had another $19.3 million worth of exercisable options when he left. He also got a pension worth at least $430,000 per year. Luter gets a one-year—renewable—$1 million consulting contract. He made $850,000 while still working. Plus perks like use of the company aircraft, an office and a secretary, cash incentive awards, health-care coverage, a cell phone, a computer, and a BlackBerry. For all this, he must work half time." (Brush, 2006)

"Brown Shoe finance chief Andrew Rosen landed a part-time consulting gig with the shoe company after he retired. He only has to work a leisurely eight days a month. As a consultant for two years, he'll get $110,417 per month, or $1.325 million a year, a 60% increase over the $829,000 in salary and bonus he received in 2005. Brown Shoe will also pick up expenses, pay a bonus, pay his medical and dental insurance, and cover his monthly dues at the St. Louis Club. What's more, his company will continue to credit his supplemental executive retirement plan as if he were an employee making $829,000 a year. Rosen also gets a pension of roughly $250,000 per year." (Brush, 2006)

"Henry Blissenbach, former president and CEO of BioScrip, continues in a one-year consulting job that will pay him $9,167 a day plus expenses. He receives the equivalent of his 2005 pay, or $550,000. But he only has to work five days a month, at most. On the way out the door, he collected $1.35 million in severance pay. The drug distribution company also agreed to pick up his family health insurance costs for two years." (Brush, 2006).

"Former First Data Chairman and CEO Charles Fote continued collecting his $91,667 each month for six months as a consultant, even though he cut back to 20% of his old work schedule. Fote also got an office, an assistant, and expenses. He received restricted stock worth $7.5 million and collected $7.9 million in long-term incentive payouts in 2003–2005." (Brush, 2006)

"Former Michaels Stores' chairman Charles Wyly, Jr., and former vice chairman Sam Wyly get a total $6 million for the next two years. The main requirement: They can't work. Charles Wyly held 4.78 million shares around the time of the Michaels Stores' buyout, which were worth $210.7 million, and Sam Wyly held 4.1 million shares worth $180.8 million." (Brush, 2006)

Corporations Don't Pay Their Fair Share

The ex-chairman of General Electric, Jack Welch, was known to be brash and outspoken. There you go again, to mimic Ronald Reagan, giving credit to a jerk for being basically a nasty human being. Now don't get me wrong, GE, as a corporate schmuck, is one of the best. Bad apple analogy, you know.

Their entire objective is to avoid taxes. They have legions of little worker bees looking for the loopholes. In 2010, they found enough loopholes to cut their tax bite to under 10%. At the time the tax rate for them would have been 35%. (Rojo, Klinger, & Anderson, 2013) That's what a couple hundred million dollars can buy—an army of lawyers and accountants to push the payment for all those roads, bridges, and schools on you.

GM, as Frank Sinatra sang, "I did it my way." They went bankrupt. This was after everyone in upper management filled their wallets and bellies, however.

During the bailout process GM received around $50 billion from the government. Shareholders and, to a limited degree, bondholders, were wiped out. Benefits remained intact, however. More's the pity since they were probably grossly inflated. Plus, I don't recall any managers losing any money or sleep. They also got a sweetheart deal from Uncle Sam. Similar to the corporate war cry that they want to keep profits yet socialize losses, GM was allowed to keep the tax losses incurred by the old GM. This in spite of different ownership, no debt remained, which was wiped out in bankruptcy, and new union contracts. Only in the United States could a totally different company get to keep the old company's write-offs. So, bye-bye taxes for years.

While diligently sweating over your own taxes and wondering just what it is that you get for that money, how does it feel to know you've been had while GE and GM find and use loopholes and pay less in taxes than you do? Or the government likes you and is breaking all the rules to make sure you survive and prosper. .

The Democrats are calling for higher taxes on the wealthy to reduce the deficit and fund spending.

The GOP wants even lower marginal tax rates for top earners, saying they fuel investment and job creation.

A study from the Congressional Research Service (CRS)—the non-partisan research office for Congress—pretty much shot holes in that long-standing Republican line. It showed that "There is little evidence over the past 65 years that tax cuts for the highest earners are associated with savings, investment or productivity growth." (Thomas, 2012) But those cuts may widen the income gap between the rich and the rest. In fact, the study found that higher tax rates for the wealthy are statistically associated with higher levels of growth. The study looked at tax rates and economic growth since 1945. "The top tax rate in 1945 was above 90 percent and fell to 70 percent in the 1960s and to a low of 28 percent in 1986. The top current ordinary income rate is 35 percent. The tax rate for capital gains was 25 percent in the 1940s and 1950s, then went up to 35 percent in the 1970s, before coming down to 15 percent —the lowest rate in more than 65 years." (Hungerford, 2012) Naturally we hear whining from the rich as it goes back to 20%. "Any and all correlations derived from reducing tax rates were not statistically significant," the study says. (Hungerford) Capital gains are defined as investment profit as opposed to income you earn from working a job (ordinary Income).

The study did say that "As top tax rates are reduced, the share of income going to the top 0.1 percent does increase, and those numbers were statistically significant." (Hungerford, 2012) So there is plenty of precedent for higher taxes in addition to the moral inequity that should be corrected.

In the 1930s, among the many issues addressed by Roosevelt was the raising of the top marginal interest rate to 90%. He was able to do that due to the extremely desperate situation of most of the population. I wonder how many of them left and gave up their citizenship? During the 1980s and 1990s, the opposite occurred as the middle class was having a decent time of it so there was a gradual reduction in tax rates. See, if you weren't so damn greedy you would help yourself even more.

There's little doubt that the many loopholes in the tax code are for the benefit of the wealthy who can afford to hire crafty lawyers and accountants. I am constantly reminded that it only takes a small spark to ignite the flames of revolt. My favorite example is the shooting of Archduke Ferdinand that started World War I. Pitchforks in Transylvania or tanks in Flanders field, makes no difference.

Tax reform could jump-start the economy. Whether it means lower rates and closed loopholes or increased rates (and closed loopholes).

It is clear that low taxes for the rich did not help or accomplish anything like creating jobs or increasing spending (they don't even spend on consumption items, they invest in gold and put the money overseas). Nothing is going into creating something through manufacturing. So much for the trickle-down theory. That's a Reagan era theory that says we will give all the money to those at the top and they will put it to work, thereby providing jobs for us at the bottom. That's working well, huh?

Do you believe they would really spend less or run away overseas if they were taxed at the level they were 30 years ago? And if by some remote chance they did, who cares? Life will go on without them and others will be given a chance to succeed. I would still confiscate their stash before they ran, however.

A double whammy, the rich are getting a bigger slice of the pie and at the same time being taxed less. Let's face it; bottom line, the rich can afford a tax increase.

As to the argument that companies should be able to pay their employees however much they please, yeah, they should be able to go broke too. Like anybody cares.

Compassionate capitalism might begin by not paying CEOs 300–400 times the income of the average hourly employee.

The CEOs job is to lie

They know how to either completely hide or at least "talk around," bad performance and overstate good performance. Distortions. Half-truths. Bending reality. "Corporate speak." Whatever you want to call it. When times are good, they lie a little. When times are bad, they lie a lot. A bunch of well-dressed whores. They have the press either in their pocket or completely bamboozled, and the public is definitely clueless no matter how many times we get burned. Maybe dumb, maybe lazy. I guess it's in our nature to look for the pony in the pile of doo doo. How this optimism compliments my position of human nature being innately less than desirable is a puzzle. There must more to it.

Several years ago Lehman Brothers had lost nearly $3 billion. Time for poster boy Richard Fuld (nice sneer on his face), Lehman's head liar, to speak with soothing forked tongue.

First, he said "This is my responsibility. We made active decisions to deploy our capital, some of which in hindsight were poor choices." (White, 2008) No crap. When I make those bad decisions I get fired or go to prison, not get a huge bonus or severance package. He then said he had "gotten the message" and was "comfortable" with Lehman's current positions. Since Fuld is not dumb, he was just a sinister liar. This was on September 10, 2008, and all is cool. On September 15, 2008, Lehman Brothers filed for bankruptcy protection. Millions of shareholders were wiped out and thousands of people lost their jobs. (White)

Granted that many of these slick shysters did go to Harvard, however, it isn't as though they came up with some brilliant tactic that no one else in the business world knew about. All they did was use leverage. Real estate buyers have been doing that for hundreds of years. Could be a minor difference is that real estate generally requires a 20% down payment. In Europe even more. These guys were using 33 to 1. That means all that has to happen is for the asset base to drop 3% and you are broke. Oh, they even lied about that as well. Said they had their own method of calculation. Come on. Is there any doubt in your mind that the lies went on right up until the morning of bankruptcy? To be fair, the real estate community got in trouble also, not only for the ridiculous rise in prices but for the high leverage. 20% as a down payment disappeared and 3% (or no percent) took its place.

Corporations can legitimately book gains as interest rates rise and therefore the principal on the bonds they owe goes down. Technically, it really is true. I'm just having trouble giving any credit to a CEO for that happening due to market circumstances.

Time and time again these snake oil salesmen CEOs claim they knew nothing about the calamity unfolding at their companies. Yet they get the big bucks. That's how stupid they think we are. As I have indicated elsewhere, they think the little guy is scum yet we're the bad guys when things go wrong. They also act like spoiled little children pouting because they couldn't have dessert. Did somebody hurt the widdle boy's feelings? They also invented the old "we get the profits and you get the losses" shuffle. Plus, truly amazing, this guy blamed everyone on the block but himself. Outside forces, whatever that is, abusive traders, false rumors, lax oversight, short sellers, and a loss of confidence by clients and other parties. Fuld at Lehman actually thought he got kicked while he was down. You can't make up that kind of logic. This guy makes the word sleazebag too positive. And being cavalier while crying foul at the same time he destroyed all those lives.

It's pretty apparent that Fuld looks down on Congress, because he thinks he is smarter than they are. He probably is, and he also knows that they are bought and paid for on both sides of the isle.

Can you say Enron, WorldCom, AIG, Countrywide?

Liars, Cheaters, Goldman

According to a study by the Stanford Institute for Economic Policy Research, California's pension shortfall is nearly 10 times worse than the official estimate of $56 billion. (Fry, 2010) Seems like someone could have seen that one coming. If you use an 8% assumption of interest rate return for your actuarial tables in an environment yielding less than a third of that, either the company will be in trouble or they will not be able to live up to their promise to their pension holders ! The point isn't the spread, it's that they, as well as many others, are losing their shirts and lying about it. Still paying those big bonuses though.

In spite of the rich capitalistic attitudes regarding free markets, there is something wrong with Goldman Sachs making obscene amounts of money while people starve. This is in addition to the fraud they perpetrated. They would have you believe making money is no crime. Well, yes it is in a zero sum environment when someone else is dying of starvation. You just killed someone, and it might have been a child. It's all about how much you get- steal a little, shame on you, steal a lot, shame on me.. And when you deliberately lie to your clients you should go to prison, no matter how many blazers you own or yachts you pilot. That's what the SEC said they did, make no bones about it. If they had just stopped after a "little fraud" we would hardly have noticed. But they can't help themselves. They want it all.

We have become immune to the avarice of salesmen. But these salesman actually lied to their clients and bet against them. Again, there are so many ways to legally screw investors, how come they went overboard? That's what is in all those red herrings, right? Just disclose and disavow and you can peddle anything. A red herring is the document in the stock market world where you divulge all the bad things you are going to do in fine print and somehow that makes everything alright.

You don't have to believe in some conspiracy theory, just understand human nature and you will agree that in order to have gotten so wealthy, most large corporations deliberately lie, cheat and steal. They are also highly leveraged, which is how in good times they make a fortune and in bad times they go broke and get bailed out by the government. Think Countrywide Financial, Washington Mutual, Lehman Brother, and Bear Stearns.

There are those who would refer back to Marx and insinuate that he would be proud that labor is reaping the benefits. What baloney. Marx would roll over in his grave if he thought labor was meant to mean those few "elites" at the top, who are getting all the money. Sure, he said that labor should receive the profit since they alone contribute value to production, but he meant the average worker, not the top management.

It is possible in our twisted and corrupt society that there is nothing illegal about these bonuses and it may even be justified by some weird capitalistic attitude, but it sure isn't ethical or moral. The only tie in to Marx here is that he would agree to just kill them. Sometimes there needs to be blood in the streets.

Many times I have conceded that we may be barking up a non-existent tree when trying to change human nature as it applies to the corporate United States and the greed of CEOs. I am reminded of the expression attributed to Mark Twain that I will twist to fit our situation. "Never try to teach ethics to a pig, it wastes your time and annoys the pig (CEO)."

In an article in a financial newsletter a few years back, Eric Fry had a pretty good parable. It went something like this: "Rain falls on the rich and the poor alike. That's symmetry. But after the rain lands, the rich receive a much larger share of the water than the poor. That's asymmetry. Some of the rich funnel as much water as possible toward their own personal reservoirs...even though they have more than enough water already. That's greed. ...And some of the rich drain the wells of their neighbors and clients to water their golf courses. That's Wall Street." (Fry, 2007) Not bad, huh?

Funny how nobody cares how much you steal when their lives are doing OK. Maybe there is a tie in there between the artificial pumping of the economy for the last decade, the complacency of the people, and the excessive greed of the Wall Street fat cats. It'll be interesting to see what happens when times turn really bad. Yeah, I can see some blood in the streets. And not the imaginary kind Andrew Carnegie or Baron Rothschild spoke of. Did you know that "the same Citigroup that lavished billions on its top employees a few years ago was the same Citibank that almost went bankrupt in the early 1990s, and was one of the chief culprits that got bailed out during the 2007 recession with tax payers' money as they got in trouble again?" (Rosenbush, 2007)

Anyone invested in the stock market should remember Wall Street is about money. It is about making as much money as humanly possible, in as many different ways as legally defensible. By the hair on their chinny chin chin. Wall Street is not about charity or altruism or the "greater good." Wall Street is a snake pit full of the worst human characteristics possible. And that's saying something. It also twists nature's law of survival of the fittest—the "fittest" being those who lie, cheat, back stab, and maneuver themselves into these obscenely overpaid positions. Only in some comic book imaginary world (the world you have allowed to exist), or maybe in raw nature, which is not man's world, do these make-believe sharks deserve that kind of money. Just remember I don't even like that lions must prey on antelope, sharks kill seals, hawks swoop up little bunnies, or a coyote gets your dog. Having lived in California, I heard about such things often. You have to wonder what kind of mind likes to repeat such stories. Because nature is set up that way, does man have to mimic it, especially for money?

I realize this harkens toward survival of the fittest and nature's way; however, I don't have to like it and I don't have to make the leap from coyotes and dogs to human beings. Isn't that what is supposed to set us apart?

Do you get the basic model for hedge funds and investment management? They make money by speculating with your money, not theirs, or by getting commissions on trading your money. You take all the risk, they get rich. Yep, the Wall Street elite get the big bucks, a disproportionate percentage of the profits. Is that the cute and cuddly word, asymmetry or is it raw greed? Morgan Stanley in 2006 had a net income of $7.4 billion while the compensation (read bonuses) for its top executives was $14.3 billion. Twice as much compensation as net income. There are numerous examples of what happens when this system goes wrong. First, nobody goes to prison. Think Barings, Societe General in Paris, JP Morgan, Bank of America,

Citicorp, etc. With all that's wrong with our society, wouldn't this be a place to start cutting back to at merely ridiculous?

Concentration of Wealth

Because the IRS does not break down income bracket any further than the top one percent that's usually what is used for comparison purposes. Better information on the top one tenth of one percent comes from private studies. The fact is, as obscene as these amounts are compared to the rest of us, they pale compared to the top of that top, the one tenth of one percent.

"All we ever hear from the Republican rich is how around half the people don't pay any taxes and the top one percent pay around 37%." (Johnston, 2011b) Those numbers are extremely misleading. Let's turn that statement around. Naturally that half doesn't pay any income tax, they don't make any money and are starving. Twenty percent of nothing is still nothing. Doesn't anyone think it sad that around half of the people in the country are in the lowest tax bracket? "When you crank up the numbers to include those citizens making up to 75,000 dollars, this collective group now pay more in taxes than the group making over one million dollars. Put another way, those in the 15% bracket pay more than those in the top 2%." (Johnston, 2011b)

Ironically, and not that anyone has any sympathy for them, the disparity between the bottom and the top of those within the one percent is just as great. "In 2009 the entry point at the bottom of the one percent rung was around $350,000. At the top of that one percent rung they were making billions! Not only do they make so much more but on average the top one tenth of one percent group only paid 18% in taxes. That's less than a taxpayer making $90,000" (Piketty, 2014)

There are those who would have you believe it's somehow OK because this has happened before, and in some cases it was even worse. How does that make me feel any better living under a bridge? Even these buffoons admit that it has been pretty one-sided since 2000.

Management and CEOs are getting rich at the expense of the worker. But you can bet the second the opportunity presents itself—meaning tight labor conditions, the employees will act with equal greed, trying to squeeze every nickel he can. No question the welfare system needs to be overhauled. It is human nature, and not very flattering, to want to get yours. It probably bears repeating the difference between welfare recipients also. Many, if not most need and deserve some help. Some, however, are just deadbeats. Even Wall Street was only getting what they could—it was the government's fault for offering. Again, the crybabies are happy to accept the government's assistance but woe is me when we want the government to put the brakes on these shysters. Then it's socialism, which according to the tainted and twisted western culture, is a bad thing. It is a little hard to sympathize with management's plight with multimillion dollar salaries and bonuses—as opposed to the 55 year old who gets fired or laid off after working for the company all her life only to be let go without a pension or severance.

Overpaying CEOs is bad business. Compensation experts Joseph Blasi and Douglas Kruse analyzed executive pay at more than 1,500 top U.S. companies between 1992 and 2002. Corporations with significantly higher than average shares of employee stock options going to the CEO and the next four top executives had lower average total shareholder returns for the decade. "Too many boards of directors think that only the top executives make a difference in the company's value, and the rest of the employees are just static factors of production like machinery," Blasi and Kruse observe. "But a growing body of evidence shows that regular employees can really make a difference." Research shows that "Broad-based stock option plans, employee ownership plans, and profit sharing plans are associated with future improvements in total shareholder return." (Morgenson, 2015)

Can anyone really lay this mockery at the feet of the "laws of supply and demand", or "their pay is determined freely by the marketplace?" I just don't know which bridge to sell you first.

Japanese and European Counterparts

In Japan, the average executive earns only 3 times as much as the average worker. In England, top executives earn 40 times as the average worker. In the United States, it's over 300 times. Are we really egotistical enough to believe a businessperson from the United States is worth 10 times as much as his English counterpart? Or 100 times his Japanese counterpart? Wow! I can't imagine any good reason why American executives earn so much more other than they are better con men. They're generally not the person responsible for output or innovation, and there is absolutely no evidence to suggest that they do better at their jobs when they are paid more. Sometimes these European bosses manage companies that are 40% bigger. CEOs in the United States make 23 times as much as CEOs in mainland China, 10 times as much as CEOs in India and 9 times as much as CEOs in Taiwan, according to a Towers Perrin worldwide survey. Taken around 2005—already obsolete as of 2013. And you know which way it has gone since then, right? European and Japanese CEOs run many of the world's leading companies for a lot less pay than Americans. U.S. CEOs make five times as much as CEOs in Spain, three times as much as CEOs France, Italy, and the Netherlands, and twice as much as CEOs in Germany and Switzerland. U.S." (Berrone, 2008) CEOs and the system have place American workers in harms way in regards to pay while managing to stay on top themselves. A horrible side effect of our outrageous practices is that the disease spreads to these other countries and there is nowhere to go and hide. The perils of globalization almost always seem to outweigh any benefits. To believe that the United States has a better gene pool shows either a lack of insight on your part, sheer stupidity, or a real propensity for prejudice. So someone is insinuating that there is a scarcity of talent in the United States? Plus I am somehow to assume the scarcity has dramatically increased over the last 30 some years, since the pay spread has gone up ten fold from 40 times the average worker in 1980 to 364 times today? Huh. Wonder where they went? I guess the exodus happened while I was at the movies.

Reuters reports, "Jiang Jianqing, chairman of Industrial and Commercial Bank of China, made just $234,700 in 2008. That's less than 2 percent of the $19.6 million awarded to Jamie Dimon, chief executive of JPMorgan Chase & Co. Three other Chinese bank CEOs also make about $230,000." (Eder, 2009) Judge for yourself.

It would appear that many people wouldn't have a problem with CEOs if we were doing better with deficits and income levels. That's probably true, given the short memories and narrow vision most of us have. That just means most of us don't know what's good for us! As Nietzsche (1876) said, "I always thought the common man should have a say until I went out among them." It would seem true that you should have focus and know what you want. The team should pull together for some common goal. We don't even have a team on the same page.

I'm thinking that's the real reason to go to Harvard. No question the Harvard Business School teaches where the money is. If it's entertainment, law, medicine, or banking—that's where you go to work. Being a hustler in and around that crowd is good, too. Their idea, by the way, of redistribution is to share among themselves. All this in addition to sitting in class next to someone whose uncle heads a major corporation.

Capitalism is supposed to be good because if you work hard you will be rewarded. What comic book have you been reading? Garbage men work hard. Ball players are merely doing what they did for fun at 11 years of age. They are just playing. They should get down on their hands and knees and thank God every day. Talent is really overrated and not worth it. Whatever happened to the gladiators idea? Let's feed them to the lions.

No Risk

There is no risk! Think of the bailouts. You need only research one industry, although it's pretty much true everywhere. Banks certainly, Wall Street—just a commission factory. AIG—see above. CEOs—lots of bonuses but never any give backs.

When times get tough and banks try to make up for their mistakes, the rich get richer. Banks tighten their credit standards far too much, forcing out not only the bad guys that deserve it but also the average person who is trying to start a business or rehab a property legitimately. And they can justify this in their own minds and on paper because it is probable, although totally unnecessary, that the rich do not only have more assets but also have better credit. Why wouldn't the rich have better credit? They don't have to scrimp and save, robbing Peter to pay Paul, and do without. There is no cushion in case of a mistake or a special need like braces or new shoes.

Simon Johnson, a professor at MIT, says, "From 1973 to 1985 the financial sector never earned more than 16% of domestic corporate profits. But in the 2000s, that figure rose to 41%." (Eder, 2009) Compensation rose along with profits and then some. Just sit around and ask yourself, how far can we push the system before it breaks?

The job description, for which these guys get paid so handsomely, isn't even the same. Banks are no longer banks, they are mortgage bankers who simply pass through loans to the secondary market. There are no more portfolio loans being made. So why pay the big bucks to CEOs, etc., when the decisions are being set by FHA, Freddie Mac, or Fannie Mae? What in the world are those CEOs doing?

The sad fact is that quantitative easing (see glossary) went to the wrong people and didn't work. There was no trickle down. Another great deal for bankers and Wall Street but not for Main Street.

Did you ever wonder what would happen if the banks were put out of business? Only stockholders, bondholders, and (definitely) executives would be wiped out, fired and put in prison. People would be brought in to replace them, and life would go on.

As I've said many times, not all people are bad and not all ideas start out bad. Time seems to twist things. I will say on that note, even though I am in favor of helping the little guy, negative amortization, which allowed an unqualified borrower to borrow more money and buy a bigger house than he should have, as an idea should have been simmered in the pot a little longer.

If you or I went into a bank and asked that our home values be tripled so we could get an addition to our credit line, would we get it? Our excuse would be,

I can't pay my bills and can't find a buyer so I have had to sell some furniture and one of the cars. The banker pretty much tells you to drop dead, for any number of reasons, good and bad. Later, the Banker goes to the Treasury and says, I can't find a buyer for any of my mortgage backed assets and the margin calls are piling up. I've nearly had to sell one of the company jets. Instead of saying drop dead, the Treasury says, we've decided to relax the rules...we're gonna let you revalue those putrid loans to whatever you want.

So why did we bother with that stupid TARP (Troubled Asset Relief Program) thing anyway? That was when the government gave the banks around 700 billion dollars to stay afloat. A lot of the banks now say they didn't even want TARP funding. Liars! The government *forced* them take the money (you know, the devil made me do it)...and then those poor top executives had to scrape by on $1 million per year (for a whole year, before starting the bonuses again). Poor babies. I'm thinking how nice it would be to get free money and guarantees and low-interest loans And how can I ever live on a mere million dollars this year, especially from a company that would have gone bankrupt without the intervention. How traumatic.

I remember being in the banking business and giving 5% on a savings account. Then we lent it to someone for 7.5%. We made money. Before that we had a system called a 3-6-3 banking rule. The bank would offer 3% interest to depositors, charge 6% on loans, and then I could be on the golf course by 3:00 pm. Now it's get free money from the government, pay little or nothing to depositors, do not lend to those who want to borrow, buy government assets with a 3% yield, and pay out huge bonuses. The too-big-to-fail scheme doesn't hurt attitudes either and further undermines any reasoning for large salaries and bonuses. It's still called hoarding and it's wrong! How can you not make money? Wait! They do actually spend some of the money on something other than themselves. They use some of it to bribe Congress. Special interests do and did just fine also.

If taxpayers support the banks, why in the world would anyone think it was OK to use that money to pay bonuses? The banks should be lending all the money to homeowners and small businesses. Fairness is a word rapidly being erased from the dictionary.

Bankers must be geniuses, they sure get paid like it. OK, I'm wrong. Geniuses don't get paid a lot of money, only salesmen and executives do. Let's not forget the only reason they are in business is that the government is guaranteeing their entire operation. Their modus operandi is to take huge risks with monumental leverage so they can pay themselves obscenely and then when it all goes South whine to the government to bail them out. Is there any wonder most

United States citizens hate bankers? They are just a bunch of chiselers. Either stupid, inexperienced, fools, and idiots or clever diabolical amoral rogues. In spite of all that the average person still puts these crooks on a pedestal. They are usually leading citizens in the community, sit on boards and contribute to political campaigns (or eventually run themselves). The lemmings actually look up to them and they are treated like priests. Well, maybe that's a bad example.

Not for a moment should you think these low lives are even in your league, let alone any better. By the way, this is called empirical knowledge, gained first hand from personal experience. What can you say when a guy is just doing his job? A detail-oriented pencil pusher. Beats me, I just know there is something wrong. The guy is a deal killer, like a lawyer without the nice suit. It's a bundle of wrongs—where family money, looks, a military attitude all combine into a personality that really doesn't have the "right stuff" or care about their fellow human beings. Forget about the exceptions I have defended many times. The fool type could be found at another bank job I had.   The money printing of the Federal Reserve is providing an unintended support to the real estate market, which benefits the rich primarily. Have you checked out the prices in San Francisco and New York lately? I recently deleted the real estate emails originating from those regions—what's the use? I can't afford it, and I can't qualify. Out in the hinterland things are still normal, at least as normal as the real estate industry can be. Much of the money, in addition to the rich here in the United States, is coming from foreign buyers with a lot of cash thanks to the lower dollar policy of the government. So, how is that helping the average U.S. citizen again? It isn't. Accounting trickery can work wonders with loopholes in the system. Either these guys are simply crooks or are really a lot smarter than I am. Even if the latter is true, history says that's a good reason to kill them and start over. That's not the kind of world I want to live in. Who do you think came up with the "Mark to Market" idea? Some accountant at Enron. Mark to Market now allows you to carry your assets at whatever high value you believe the market will bear, backed up by a bogus appraisal. You used to have to carry assets at the lower of cost or value. Oh, and how cool is it when the guy at the top getting all that money says he either doesn't know what is going on or he doesn't understand it? Then how did he ever get that job? And why are we paying him? Ken Lay, of Enron fame, said he had so much information he didn't know what to do with it all. His argument was that he couldn't be guilty of misleading investors if he didn't understand it or didn't know what was going on himself. Bernie Ebbers at WorldCom used the same legal line. Ebbers, you will no doubt recall, went even farther, using the, "I'm just a dumb country boy" routine. There has to be something to the saying that, "if it's too complicated there's something wrong, or, simply don't do it."

Not to be outdone, the legal boys are hard at it also. You have to be truly amazed at how those in power in the financial industry consistently avoid criminal charges and end up paying only pennies on the dollar in a civil suit. There seems to be little incentive to do the right thing in corporate world when the fine is quite a bit less than the profit made. Bank of America paid around 16 billion for a trillion dollar screw up, Chase paid 13 billion in fines for a 450 billion dollar chunk of business and Citigroup paid 7 billion for their mess. Plus they don't have to admit they did anything wrong! (Grossman, Rexrode, & Fitzpatrick, 2014).

Clever lawyers now suggest the "Deferred Prosecution Agreement" be applied to the big banks. It started out as a way to deal with juveniles and minor drug offenders. If the defendants didn't get into any trouble for a specified period of time, the prosecution would be deferred and ultimately just dropped The Department of Justice is in the case, trying to prevent such chicanery. (Chung, 2015). And you thought crime didn't pay. Tsk, tsk.

You Don't Even Have To Succeed

All of the examples cited seldom differentiate between good and bad CEOs and their pay. If you are at the top, you can fail miserably in corporate America and still leave with a lot of money. Scott Livengood received $46,000 per month consulting for Krispy Kreme, the doughnut company, after tremendous losses. Franklin Raines was booted out of Fannie Mae, but he still gets $114,000 per month in pension benefits. (Pizzigati, 2007)

Remember Carly Fiorina who was sacked and received $42 million for doing a lousy job for Hewlett Packard in 2005? (LaMonica, 2005) Now she gets paid who knows what to be a political pundit on television.

No Accountability

Most corporations, and especially those in the banking industry and on Wall Street, could use a good shower. Or maybe I need one after reading about their antics. How about a good laugh? Let's call it self-governing. Are you really nuts? People in positions of power and responsibility need to be held accountable for their actions and especially for their part in the 2006–2011 recession. These people are parasites living off the sweat of the workers and feeding at the trough for their own benefit. Instead of hiding behind the corporate entity, some individuals need to take responsibility and a good place to start would be the boards of directors.

For whatever reason, probably to encourage business by protecting the higher up individual, the corporate entity was born. Most likely it was a good idea in the beginning, but naturally it got exploited. Corporations were formed as legal entities that serve as a structure for aggregating capital and engaging in commerce. Sounds simple enough. Then the owners (stockholders) select people to run things. In public companies CEOs and presidents get a lot of attention (because they get paid excessively and cheat a lot), but the boards of directors supposedly hold all the power, even if they either don't use it or abuse it. Shareholders vote on who gets elected to these positions (supposedly to protect their interests), but unfortunately management typically recommends a slate of candidates to choose from, and it is impossible and very expensive to get a slate of your own up for vote.

Directors are supposed to be the watchdogs, overseeing the CEOs, presidents, and generally the activities of the companies they serve. When it comes to big companies, directors tend to have very impressive resumes, which sound good in theory but do not mean a heck of a lot in practice. Is this back to human nature again, and that "absolute power corrupts absolutely?" So, if they have all this power, why aren't they accountable? They also get paid excessively. Let's see. They get paid handsomely, and it's their job to protect the owners, what's wrong here? These people, like the CEOs and other executives, get paid millions even when the corporation loses millions. Seriously? And to add injury to insult they all required bailouts from the government at taxpayer expense and yet no one went to prison. Let's just say the recession was no one's fault for a fantasy moment. Why would you pay them extravagantly or give them bonuses? Does anyone really think, with the insider good old boy network in place, these guys didn't have any insight into the potential problems? So, it's either woeful mismanagement, or they're just self-serving crooks. Some choice.

To really make a mess, why not add a few politicians to the mix? We are creating a nation of cynics, and if not, we should be. Cynicism should be the prerogative of academics. You'll know compensation policies have changed for the better if CEO pay goes down while worker pay goes up.

Lest we seem to pick on the management side too much, let us not forget the union mafia, which started out with so much promise and ended up being human as well.

Ought to Be in Prison

Why aren't the guys who constantly rape, pillage, and steal from the rest of us, and who caused the credit-crisis, in prison? Not much of a Horatio Alger story here. So much for good examples for our kids, who now believe it's OK to lie, cheat, and steal, especially if you can do it under the guise of corporate legitimacy. Instead, they get lucrative book deals on top of the millions they stole from us. Golden-parachuting bailout bandits is how I heard them described.

If these guys didn't violate any laws, then the laws should be changed—retroactively. I'm guessing they all flunked Ethics 101. The test, as I understand it from a legal standpoint, is whether or not they knew or should have known at the time they made decisions that the decision would "more probably than not" cause harm. You can't even get these amoral sociopaths to admit they did anything wrong. Let us not forget that one of the really stomach churning or laughable responses we get from these cockroaches is that they didn't know what was going on. I guess they never heard President Harry Truman's remark "The buck stops here." I would be ashamed to ever admit I didn't know what was going on in my company. But then again, I'm not amoral or facing criminal charges (not that anything will ever come of it). There is civil law precedent that contains "look back" clauses that could indeed make these crimes retroactive.

Part of the problem is that most of Congress is so completely oblivious to how the rest of us actually live that they weren't even aware there was a problem. The vast majority of Congress just isn't as smart as I would like them to be, considering that many, if not most, are lawyers. It seems they just can't keep up with Wall Street.

Since the average Joe is being asked to shoulder the burden and belly up to the table to contribute, maybe these top executives, who have made hundreds of millions of dollars over the years, could voluntarily give some of it also.

Front running on insider information

This book has as one of its main goals, the thought that many of the rich don't even desire a decent living, let alone the tremendous rewards they receive. One debate that is amusing, but almost impossible for anyone to win, is who is more greedy and more corrupt, Washington or Wall Street. Also, how in the world do they do it? Front running on insider information seems to be a trait instilled firmly in both camps. We are really fortunate to have so much corruption to choose from.

The high frequency computer trading by the big guys on Wall Street is set in place and doesn't even require any thought. Just get in and get out by sandwiching yourself in the middle. "High-frequency trader guys have computers with cables hooked right into the exchange. They are able to see what you want to buy, slip in the middle, and buy the shares of IBM before you can. They then sell the shares you originally wanted for one-tenth of a penny higher and make a sliver of profit. They do this on millions of trades a day, pocketing fractions of a penny on every trade." To make matters worse, the fee structure destroys the announced return to the investor. The average returns of Hedge Funds from 2004 to 2014, was 6.53%, according to the Barclay Hedge Fund Index. But wait! Unlike the shill hawking his or her wares on TV throwing in an extra bottle of whatever, hedge funds dip in and take more out. Their compensation package, which makes them gazillionaires, is call 2/20. This means they get 2% off the top and 20% of any profits. No loss in any down year mind you. So, immediately knock off 2% each year for management fees leaving only 4.53%. Then, assuming the Fund made over 5%, they get another 20%. Most hedge funds guarantee that they won't charge the extra fee unless they return more than 5% on your money. But they, unlike even the evil IRS, charge the 20% on the entire 6.53%, not the amount above the 5% and not after taking their fee of

2%. Now that 6.53% return is down to around 3.23%. Bummer. (Altucher, 2015)

As to the guys and gals on Capitol Hill, for a few years after things went bad after 2007, congressmen's net worth were up 30% per year. Now that even the average consumer has regained his money, can you imagine how much the congressmen have made? Mitch McConnell's net worth jumped almost 30 percent in 2013 alone. The guy is supposedly worth over $12 million all the while opposing minimum wage increases, fighting unemployment insurance extensions and supporting tax breaks that send jobs overseas. How can he sleep at night? Kay Hagan's net worth increased 37 percent during the two years of her first Senate term. Senator Johnny Isakson's assets more than doubled in value in 2013. Did your nest egg? How do you suppose this can happen? Boy, these people really are brilliant investors. Even if our politicians aren't directly investing on inside information, they are still being paid millions of dollars by hedge funds. In 2009, former secretary of the Treasury Larry Summers was paid $5.2 million in compensation from the hedge fund D.E. Shaw, plus hundreds of thousands of dollars in speaking fees at financial institutions like Goldman Sachs, Merrill Lynch, and Lehman Brothers. (Altucher, 2015)

There is little doubt, as mentioned many times, that it's hard to cure an ill when you have to go through the perpetrator to get it done. The crimes committed by these felons are mostly legal, because the felons passed the laws making them legal. Our democratic system allows wealthy individuals and corporations to buy votes from congressmen with legal bribes. These votes get them tax breaks, subsidies, and favorable legislation on whatever their needs are. Apparently, even the Supreme Court, (packed politically) is in on it. Because of interpretations by the court, corporations can now "threaten" elected officials through putting up money in opposition. The court ruled that this money was the same as "free speech". (Johnston, 2003) (Johnston, 2011c) I couldn't make this up if I tried. You can find all the articles you want stating, that "it's for the good of the country."

On November 13th of 2011 60 minutes aired a segment based on a book by Peter Schweizer of the far-right Hoover Institution. According to Politico, "Schweizer was a speech-writing consultant for former President George W. Bush and helped write a book with conservative commentator Glenn Beck. He is also listed as the editor of website run by conservative journalist Andrew Breitbart." These credentials are major, major red flags on a person's credibility. In spite of that the segment was fairly unbiased. (Johnston, 2011c). The accusations from the report include:

- Representative Spencer Bachus (R-AL) trading in funds that would make money if the economy tanked after receiving secret briefings warning of the pending collapse of the financial sector;

- Speaker John Boehner (R-OH) "just days before the [public option] provision was publicly killed off, Boehner bought health care stocks, all of which went up."

IPOs are another way for insiders to be enriched. An IPO occurs when a company goes public. People, like politicians owed favors, who get in on the ground floor of an IPO that is undervalued will make a killing. Former House Speaker Nancy Pelosi and her husband have participated in at least eight IPOs. In the 2008 VISA IPO, Pelosi was working on legislation that would affect credit cards at the time. In the '90s former House Speaker Tom Foley (D-Washington) participated in 42 of these special-access IPOs. Former New York Sen. Alfonse D'Amato (R-New York) was also granted access to IPOs. D'Amato received this special stock from a firm that was under investigation by a Senate committee on which D'Amato was the chairman at the time. That's gotta be alright, right?

The fact that members of Congress and their staff - and any government employee, for that matter - are allowed to own and/or trade in stocks at all leaves wide open the perception if not the actual fact that they can use information that is not available to others for personal enrichment. (Johnston, 2011c)

There are many ways to buy votes. Howard Hughes was rumored to have bribed with land and Dennis Hastert bought land in the path of progress, then he voted on a highway going close to it. When Illinois Congressman Dennis Hastert became speaker of the House in 1999, he was worth a few hundred thousand dollars. He left the job eight years later a multi-millionaire. (Johnston, 2011c) That's just coincidence, right?

Finally there is what's called the Revolving Door, in which government employees are promised lucrative future jobs. At several times their current pay. Gee, who wouldn't bend over backwards to do favors for their future employer? Not only does the company get anything it wants but the employee will spend time thinking of other ways to help as well. At least 40% of congressmen and their help make the move to lobbyist. (Johnston, 2011c)

Supposedly there is a rule that you have to sit out a year before lobbying. Bob Livingston showed us how to get around that- just hire underlings and tell them what to do. Then there was Rep. Billy Tauzin who as chairman of the committee in the House that regulates the pharmaceutical industry, pushed through the Medicare prescription drug program that was so beneficial to the pharmaceutical industry. He then retired and took a job as head of the pharmaceutical lobbying group, the Pharmaceutical Research and

Manufacturers of America (Public Citizens Congressional Watch, 2005)

Regardless of the legality of all of this, there has to be a way to stop it. A simple rule prohibiting government workers from jumping ship for more money? Why not? How about simply no trading in any kind of stocks at all while a public official? Not even through your "Blind Trust." Stop allowing corporate money to influence government decisions and individuals. Difficult? Sure. Impossible? No way.

Although the American culture encourages greed and corruption under the guise of capitalism, we are not alone. Greedy people find a nest almost everywhere, including a Communistic country like China. Here are a few of the more outrageous examples:

"Zhou Yongkang, a prior member of the Politiburo Standing Committee and also national police chief. He stole over 16 billion in cars, paintings, cash, securities, gold and silver. **General Xu**, formerly the vice chairman of China's Central Military Commission, was found guilty of taking bribes for promoting people. He lived in a 21,000 square foot mansion, had all the same goodies. **Liu Zhijun** was the Minister of the National Ministry of Railways. He was sentenced to death. It seems like the punishment doesn't always fit the crime, although that might have something to do with who you know also. **Gu Junshan**, a Lieutenant

General in the military was arrested in early 2012 after his suspected involvement in a massive scheme that involved the sale of military appointments. The sales totaled over 5 billion Yuan. **Wei Pengyuan**, deputy chief of the coal bureau at the National Energy Administration, has been charged with taking $5.8 million in bribes from 2002 to 2012. **Ma Chaoqun** wasn't even a big wig. He was a mid-level water-supply official who allegedly used his position to steal a bundle. Thought to be in the neighborhood of $163 million." (Jacobs, 2015). Chicken feed. What a great country. And all under a communist regime.

CHAPTER ELEVEN - WHAT THEY THINK

Just the Hired Help

This is nothing more than the hired help we're talking about. Just like the woman who turned down $2 to sleep with someone, but accepted $500,000 for the same act. We know exactly what she is, we're just negotiating the price. No matter how naïve one is, one should be able to see that the money used to pay these jerks has to come from somewhere, and that somewhere is usually from lowly employees or the shareholders. We all know how the system works. First of all, there is no risk, you either get a ridiculous amount if you do well or you get just a great salary (probably 10 times the average pay) if you fall on your face. In fact, it's likely that you get an outrageous bonus even if you fall on your face. You never have to give back any of the bonus from last year or pay a penalty for poor performance this year. This system is so flawed I can't even write about it without getting angry. There is no economic justification for these high amounts. There is no human being that much better than the rest, no matter if he is a CEO, a football player, or a movie star. I'm giving the benefit of the doubt here. Quite frankly, most of these people shouldn't be allowed to use public toilets.

"Never in the history of Wall Street have so many earned so much in so little work and time, said

Eric fry, referring to the $36 billion in year-end bonuses that Goldman Sachs, Morgan Stanley, Merrill Lynch, Lehman Brothers, and Bear Stearns gave to its employees at the end of 2006." (Fry, 2007b) "I've already mentioned some of the distasteful facts surrounding these antics. At least they did make a profit that year. But they outdid themselves in 2007, when these same bloodsuckers lost money yet raised the amount of bonuses to $38 billion in year-end bonuses. Why do they do this? Because they can get away with it. Everyone is either in cahoots, has another agenda, or is stupid. Sanctions (penalties for doing bad things) imposed by the Securities and Exchange Commission in fiscal 2007 fell to the lowest level since 2002 and the collected amount is down by half." (Fry) Do you think the SEC is in the hip pockets of Wall Street? Whatever the answer, the question should be asked.

No company should be setting aside that large of a percentage of its net revenue to compensate one person and no company should be paying out 50% of its net revenue for bonuses as a whole. Why? Because it is taking money away from shareholders, customers, and maybe even the community. To say that the compensation is agreeable to the shareholders does not take into account the system of corporate monopolies. These guys are insulated from shareholders and any repercussions. One would think that being a public company, if shareholders want to give their CEO $64M, let them do it. But I seriously doubt that they wouldn't rather have the money themselves instead. In many cases, there is simply no choice for the customer.

There's also the issue of corporate responsibility to its clients, when a company grows to that size.

I wonder if these "too big to fail" banks shouldn't be broken apart to create more efficiency and more competition.

These snakes would have gone bankrupt if public money had not bailed them out.

To pay people to churn accounts and markets without really producing anything is debatable to begin with. Besides, the money stays mainly on the plain, meaning the shysters are heavily involved in the churn. Churning is merely buying and selling a customer's portfolio to make commissions while not really making any money for that customer.

If you as an investor disagree with their pay packages, don't invest; vote with your dollars.

If there are no "superstars" available (debatable as to whether there is such a thing and if so, what are they really worth), or the applicants say they can get a better deal elsewhere, wish them well and say good-bye. It won't take long to see whether or not all these businesses will fail because they don't have some overpaid schmuck at the top.

The President of the United States only receives $400,000 a year, how can you justify paying a mere CEO more? We're not here to debate whether or not he's actually worth it. When you get right down to it, what's the difference between Wall Street and the drug dealers? Better suits? Not even that. Since they both destroy peoples' lives, perhaps they should be roommates at Sing Sing.

Shouldn't these CEOs have to pay into the kitty if they lose money? After all, the shareholders do.

The tax code should be changed so that any compensation paid to the highest paid execs that is in excess of a certain ratio to the compensation paid to the lowest paid employees would no longer be deductible by the company. That is what the tax code used to provide until it was overhauled in 1986—and executive compensation has steadily exploded ever since. Actually, I take that back. Let's simply take all of the money the CEOs were given over and above the ratio and triple penalize the corporation.

Wall Street elite believe that "what's yours is mine and what's mine is mine." The connection between merit and pay disappeared a long time ago. Bloomberg said it nicely, "Wall Street bonuses possess a distinct upward bias." (Crotty, 2009) Billions of dollars are being lost yet billions are also being given to millionaire employees. That does not seem to be good business.

Just for kicks, let's ask ourselves, "How much is $38 billion?" Bloomberg again chimed in with the following: it is more money than Wall Street's five largest brokerage firms—combined—earned during that same 12 month period. $38 billion is also more than the combined earnings of these five firms during all of 2004 *and* 2005. It is more than the annual GDP of Guatemala or Costa Rica. It is seven times more than the annual budget of the National Cancer Institute (NCI), America's principal agency for cancer research. It is three times more money than the entire world spends on humanitarian aid, twice the amount necessary to provide basic health care to every child in the world, and three times the sum necessary to provide clean drinking water to every child in the world." (Wiggins & Mathius, 2007) In my opinion, it would be a toss-up as to which is the bigger travesty, CEO pay or the money wasted on wars. In that regard, it is worthwhile remembering some of the costs and comparisons, especially some fine statistics given by Dwight David Eisenhower. Eisenhower said, "Every gun that is made, every warship launched, every rocket fired takes money from those who are going hungry, cold and are not clothed, He went on to say, " War wastes labor, lives and scientific experimentation (even though proponents will point to the progress and inventions made during war time) and diminishes hope. As of 1953, The cost of one modern heavy bomber is this a modern brick school in more than 30 cities. It is two electric power plants, each serving a town of 60,000 population. It is two fine, fully equipped hospitals. It is some 50 miles of concrete highway. We pay for a single fighter plane with a half million bushels of wheat. We pay for a single destroyer with new homes that could have housed more than 8,000 people. That is more money than a man earning ten thousand dollars every year is going to make in his lifetime." (Schlesinger, 2011). Naturally all the costs and prices have gone up considerable but the ratios still hold.

It's not just the money stolen from shareholders, employees, and the community, it's the attitude it cultivates—that of risk taking without risk and the establishment of huge social and monetary gaps. Don't kid yourself into thinking that won't end badly, even if it takes a long time. Someone will pay dearly for this mistake.

Obscene CEO and other executive pay pretends that unbridled greed is "merit-based pay." To these people, an extra $10 million is just a game or a scorecard while millions are either starving or scraping by month to month. How quickly we forget that these people are merely employees of a company owned by shareholders. Words like audacious, outrageous, disgusting, reprehensible, over-the-top, and rapacious wouldn't begin to describe the culture here in this country. You cannot possibly believe that kind of behavior and remuneration can continue without repercussions. A corrupt society always fails, it just seems to take a long time. That kind of disparity leads to French Revolutions, as well it should. Keep it up and at some point, we the lemmings will revolt and either you will be stripped of your possessions or killed.

Don't you just love it when these guys are disappointed because they only got a 3 million dollar bonus? The papers are full of reports that bonuses will plummet. I don't get it. Instead of plummeting to just astronomical here are two other options. No bonus at all, or the greedy SOBs have to pay some back! So, let me see if I have this right. The government gives them my money (taxes) to pay bonuses to retain "superstars." As stated many times, all you have to do is have everyone stop paying them so much and they will have nowhere to jump ship. This is the same argument and solution found under the "tax the rich" section. Half of these guys are still wet behind the ears at 27 years of age. They should get down on their knees and thank God that they have a job. They also believe bonuses are automatic, and they are "entitled" to them. There is no question that money brings out the greed in most people. In fact, I hear that as a justification all the time. "You would do the same thing in my shoes." Well, you can't blame me, we all do it, if given the opportunity." Makes me sick. Am I just jealous? Why sure. So what? What's that got to do with it anyway? Time for a plug again. The only way this will stop is someone will have to die. Thank you Mr. Marx. Don't feel too bad for the family these schmucks leave behind either, most of them are never home, are cheating on their wives (their wives are mere trophy wives anyway who never worked a day in their lives), and are estranged from their children.

Who Is The Big Cheese?

It would appear there is a difference of opinion as to who is the big cheese in a public company. Stakeholders covers a wide range of individuals. The question is what do you want from your society? What is the purpose of a company? On the one side there are those who are dyed-in-the-wool capitalists who think the first and only reason for being in business is to make as much money as is humanly possible, at any expense. If you don't feel at least a little twinge of discomfort at that statement we are probably done here. That side of the debate believes that the CEOs and other upper management run the company and the world—and the heck with everyone else. These folks believe they are the lords of the manor and the rest of us are mere serfs.

Instead of coming up with an excuse as to why it's OK to be a greedy jerk, why not figure out a way to change human nature? Granted that's virtually impossible so we move to phase two, which would be put in place some guidelines and severe punishments. Over time they'll get the point. You might even consider rewarding something else besides bad behavior leading to profits like good work and a job well done. There is at least a possibility that this overpaying of people and the greed accompanying it are at least partially to blame for the corrupting, crippling, and slow decline of the United States. We constantly hear haranguing against the entitlement attitude within the welfare system for the poor. Isn't this CEO debacle the same entitlement attitude? They're not entitled to multimillion dollar bonuses. They are nothing more than employees of companies that are owned by someone else.

And please don't go to the mat with the speculation that "They will leave and then woe is me, who will run our company?" There are so many answers to that I don't know where to begin. First of all—let em! Where are they going to go—France, Germany, England, or China? Nobody pays the ridiculous amounts we do. And that's assuming we can't spread the controls to other countries as well as all across the United States. Whew! Back from the rant, at least consider that some of that money given to the greedy SOBs could be set aside and used when the next crisis hits. I suspect, if given the chance, there are an abundance of people who would be willing and able to take over the reins. Even if it took a bit of training. Look at the track records. Not only is it wrong to pay these people huge golden parachutes when fired, the fact is they were fired because they couldn't do the job. Incidentally, if the guy can't do the job for one million, what makes you think they can do it for ten million? Were they somehow not working up to par at one million?

That brings up the psychological theories that it would be just wonderful for all of us if we could work at something we really loved. Taking that to its logical conclusion, let's assume these schmucks love what they do. Are you telling me they, if they only get $300,000 per year, will leave the profession to be a carpenter, taxi driver, or dog walker?

Think for a moment just how much money we are talking about. Over 350 times the average worker. Is there any justification for that kind of money difference? What kind of rationale says certain human beings are that much better than others? Yet, that is exactly what is being said. Workers in the United States, according to one study, whether you hold it as gospel or not, were second only to Norway in productivity. But these workers do not reap the benefits of their productivity. It goes to the top executives. "Top executives at large U.S. companies averaged eleven million dollars in 2014." (Mishel & Davis, 2015) That was based on the average worker making $16 per hour.

Need I stir the fires again by adding that some didn't
even turn a profit for their companies? Even if I lost
the battle about their worth, if the end result was
negative, how can that be justified? Just a few more
facts to choke on: "In 2007 the bosses at the top 20
investment shops earned an average of $657.5 million
for the year, according to data cited by the "Executive
Excess 2007" report." (Anderson, Cavanaugh, Collins,
& Pizzigati, 2007)We haven't learned anything in one
hundred years. Yet all we hear about is how minimum
wage will destroy our society.

   Most of these numbers don't even count the
benefits and perks. "According to the 'Corporate
Library,' CEOs at S&P 500 companies retire with an
average of $10.1 million in their supplemental
executive retirement plans." (Anderson, Cavanaugh,
Collins, & Pizzigati, 2007) Remember these figures
are from reports in 2007. Some of these benefits are
personal travel using corporate jets, reimbursement for
taxes on bonuses and stock options, and payment of
country club fees. Tough life. As always, these
numbers may seem somewhat confusing due to
averaging. When that happens the average is skewed
because the rich have so much more and theirs makes
the averages seem higher. That means the middle-class
households having much less even than the numbers
indicate. The wealthy hold most of these assets. "As of
2013, the top 20 percent of working-age households by

income owned 67.7 percent of all retirement account assets, while the bottom 50 percent owned only 7.4 percent. Among older households, a study for the Social Security Administration found that only 19 percent of families headed by a person over age 65 were actually receiving distributions from a retirement account as of 2009, with only 8 percent of families in the bottom income quartile receiving any such distributions." (Miller, Madland, & Weller, 2015)

CHAPTER TWELVE – TRICKSTERS!

Board Members

As stated many times, you put the responsibility for pay increases in the hands of other CEOs from other companies (board members) and you are just asking for trouble—or should I say corruption. Cozy is the word that comes to mind. It's "I want what Harry makes," not how did I do this year? Plus the consulting firms that advise companies on CEO pay have either no incentive to be fair or recommend higher pay packages because they get a percentage and also get paid for doing other consulting jobs for the same company.

This gets even worse. If you look through proxy statements of several of these large corporate boards, you'll find something very interesting. Some of these guys are on more than one board. First of all, that's probably a conflict of interest. Second, all of these jobs are part-time so how good of a job can they be doing? By the way, "part-time pays about $250,000 per year per company. Plus expenses no doubt. Example: James Cash, a Harvard Professor, serves on the boards of GE, Chubb Insurance, and Walmart. Mr. Cash earned $812,915 in compensation in 2011 from all three." (Johnson R. , What Occupy Wall Street SHOULD Have Said, 2013). Most board members are recommended by other board members and/or management. Not very arm's length.

If you aren't going to do the job of governing the company, overseeing management, and protecting shareholders, then what element of the position of director is so important that it should go to people who serve on lots of other boards? (Johnson R. , What Occupy Wall Street SHOULD Have Said, 2013). I'll bet I could have run a few companies into the ground just as well as they did in the last recession for a lot less money, too. Think General Electric, General Motors, Citi, AIG, Bank of America, Fannie Mae, Freddie Mac, and most of the top banks who had to be bailed out.

Lee Raymond, former chief executive of ExxonMobil, walked away with a $400 million retirement package (see appendix C). Outgoing United Health Group CEO William McGuire got an estimated $1.1 billion retirement package when he steps down. Richard Grasso of the New York Stock Exchange got a $180 million retirement package when he stepped down in 2003." (Brush, 2006)

Can anything ever be done to cure this? Probably not, short of blood in the streets. Is there a plan? Sure. Close the loopholes that let companies deduct executive pay defined as a performance incentive. Tax all earnings as ordinary income instead of capital gains. Limit the amount of income execs can roll tax free into their retirement plans just like the rest of us.

Make it easier for shareholders to elect who they select for board members. Or perhaps set up some requirements that these board members be a lot more arm's length. Make them responsible for profits and all other aspects of a corporation. Just maybe you might get more than a management lapdog. No up-front bonuses to come on board. No severance pay, especially if fired. No consulting gigs after leaving, just a non-compete clause.

How can life be that unfair? Why do CEOs get paid handsomely even when they fail? Chalk it up to contacts. Stack the board with your pals who will give you anything you want, knowing that next week you will be on their board and do the same for them. The stock options are not the problem, it's that the goals are set too low with little incentive and almost an automatic given that they will pay off. Performance targets are set so low so low even a monkey could pass. "There is no penalty for failure, only reward for success." (Norris, 2007). The words arm's length don't even enter the picture when the board is made up of fellow CEOs with a vested interest in seeing amounts go up and maybe have the benefit of that same CEO being on their board later.

Sometimes the CEO is also the Chairman of the Board. The boss of the board evaluating his pay. Huh? How is that for convoluted graft and corruption?

(Wirtz, 2006) I wonder if they at least excuse themselves when the vote gets to them?

Richard Parsons

"Time Warner said in regard to Mr. Parsons, his bonus was linked to financial performance of the company in areas like revenue, free-cash-flow growth, and reductions in debt." (Ames, 2012) That sounds like a combination of doublespeak and shear baloney.)

Parsons is another one with a track record of failure.

At Time Warner Parsons engineered the deal widely considered the "single worst business deal in corporate American history: a fraud-rife merger that wiped out $200 billion in shareholder value, ruined employees, retirees and investors, sparked numerous criminal investigations and dozens of lawsuits, and yet somehow managed to enrich a tiny handful of executives—including Dick Parsons—to the tune of hundreds of millions of dollars." (Ames, 2012). Parsons prepped well for the Time Warner fiasco. "Through the mid-1990s, Parsons served as chairman of Dime Savings, the Northeast's poster child for savings & loan criminal fraud. Dime turned out to be the New England region's closest equivalent to Charles Keating's Lincoln Savings down in Arizona, a giant criminal fraud mill with victims ranging from gullible low-income home buyers to entire regional economies laid waste to the fraud-pumped housing bubble." (Ames) In spite of all the criminal wrongdoings, Parsons got away with it. I guess this is where he got his ideas on how to run Citi into the ground later. But Parsons was just getting warmed up. He then moved on to Citigroup where he laid waste to anything that would burn. After two horrendous failures, to whom did this come as a surprise? They should teach this in all management classes as how to get ahead. Everywhere this guy goes there are lawsuits, huge executive payouts and company failures. "At Citi he arranged a pay package for CEO Vikram Pandit amounting to $53 million despite the fact that Citi's stock plummeted 44% in 2011." (Ames)

Parson's qualifications? Let's see, he dropped out of high school with a "C" average, later earning a GED certificate. At college he joined a frat, and became the guy who's at the bar all the time. He flunked out of college. He's a frat-boy slacker- the typical qualifications for a one percenter. Somehow he got in the pockets of the Rockefeller clan. Contacts, my man, contacts. Even though it was initially merely as the son of the Rockefeller groundskeeper, that was enough. He was under the protective wing. Whether he was really smart or not is up for debate. Some say yes, others say "isn't it a coincidence that he got into Albany Law School without any undergraduate degree while Nelson Rockefeller was Governor in Albany? Isn't it a coincidence that he did so well on the bar exam while Harry Albright (a Rockefeller crony) was in charge of scoring the exam, Oh yeah, and Harry Albright was later head of Dime savings and appointed Parsons to replace him. (Ames) Once when asked how he could sleep at night, Albright said "I am entirely unapologetic." (Ames) After Dime, Nelson's brother Lawrence Rockefeller got into the act, appointing Parsons to board positions at Freddie Mac, Fannie Mae, Citigroup and Time Warner. (Ames)

This section on Parsons may be a bit long in the tooth but the game plan could be applied to most of the CEOs, which is why it's worthwhile.

Still liars figure and figures lie. Given the below-average performance of the stock, it's safe to conclude that those targets were set low enough for a baboon to be able to make them. The board (self-serving right wingers) also states it has been rewarding Parsons for achievements like better relations with shareholders and the press, attracting strong managers, increasing diversity and "Articulating the company's strategy of operating its businesses as best in class." (Ames, 2012) Whatever that means. I thought that's what he was getting paid for in the first place, you know, doing his job.

These guys at Time Warner are just too good to be true. They're the gift that keeps on giving. After

Parsons, Time Warner appointed Robert Marcus as CEO in 2014. After only a few months he negotiated the sale of the company. Since he sold the company right out from under not only the workers, who get nothing except unemployment, but himself, he got to take home $80 million. Only in America can one think that's fair and reasonable. Just one example. The same thing goes everywhere. Coca Cola plans on giving senior management $13 billion over the next four years. For simplicity that's around 3 billion a year. It would take the average $50,000 a year worker twenty years to earn one million dollars. A billion is one thousand times that! That's twenty thousand years! Times 3 billion is sixty thousand years. If I had sixty thousand years I bet I could get their job done. You could learn a lot in sixty thousand years. GM, the people that make a second rate automobile and brought you disaster a few year back, will be paying their CEO 14 million a year. Do I need to do the math again?

For these no risk, big reward jobs, the only excuse the board can come up with is "Our compensation falls within the normal ranges observed at companies with similar revenue and business lines." (Johnson R. , 2014) So, "everybody does it" is the excuse you are falling back on? Gee, my Mom told me that was no excuse when I was eight years old. Oh, excuse me I need to get ready for my golf game with the CEO I just gave all that money to because he will be returning the favor when discussion of my pay rate comes up at my company.

Stock Buy-Backs

All in the name of good business practices. That's the company line espoused by CEOs when questioned about having their hand in the till. Stock buy backs are an example of this. CEOs would have us believe that buybacks are good for the company, and you as the shareholders. In some respects that might be true. If you have nowhere else to put the money, maybe. But then, what are we paying you for if not to come up with good ways to allocate cash? Perhaps if the stock has gone down and now seems a great buy? Again, maybe. But just to pump the price up since the same earnings spread over fewer shares of stock would make you look good, hit your bonus numbers or give you an opportunity to dump some shares- not so much, Shylock. Example: If a company's net income was $100 million and it had 50 million shares outstanding, the company earned $2 per share. Now the company earnings stayed flat at $100 million. By repurchasing 10 million shares, there are now 40 million shares outstanding. By dividing the shares into the earnings (40 million into $100 million) EPS would equal $2.50, meaning it grew 25%. Not bad when you didn't earn a penny more than last year. If the CEO receives a bonus based on EPS growth, he or she is going to have a lot of incentive to make sure each dollar of net income goes further. They can accomplish this by reducing the number of shares outstanding - regardless of whether it's a good deal for shareholders. Or perhaps they get a bonus based on share price. By juicing the EPS, the stock price could go higher. (Litchenfield, 2015)

Marisa Mayer at Yahoo sold 793,000 shares while steering a stock repurchase of the company for 3.1 billion dollars! The stock was at double its five year average so why the buy back? Estee Lauder CEO Fabrizio Freda had the company buy back $2.3 billion worth of stock at twice the P/E it could have been bought at over the last 12 months. Meanwhile Fabrizio sold $6.4 million for himself. The best you could say is he can do whatever he wants. It might even be termed Financial Engineering, making it sound as though there is something cleaver in all this. At some point you need to ask yourself the burning question, "is this the kind of world I want to live in." Some fairly shrewd people like Carl Icahn, among many others, say the money should be used to buy or upgrade plants, or equipment or pay dividends. Makes sense to me. To put some numbers to this chicanery, companies are buying back shares at a valuation on average today of 22 versus an historical average of 15. That's 38% higher. If they had really been cleaver they would have been buying back in 2009 when their stock was really low. (Litchenfield, 2015)

CHAPTER THIRTEEN - SUMMARY

There is plenty of indisputable evidence that the rich are getting richer, in no small part because of the Federal Reserve's inflationary and foolhardy policy. Forget about whether or not it's deliberate, it's the wrong thing to do and it is destroying lives.

Capitalists Verses Workers

Thomas Piketty, in his 2014 bestselling book entitled *Capital in the Twenty-First Century*, is clearly a liberal—in all the right ways—yet some still believe him wrong in that the working man and the investing man are at odds in a capitalistic society. Personally, I think he hit the nail on the head. He believes the working man always gets the worse end of the deal. He's right again. Bear in mind there are 30 million people who disagree—some of whom don't even have ulterior motives. The rate of widening of the gap between the rich and the rest of us is up for debate but not the widening.

In a normal business arrangement—say a real estate deal—the money partner (capitalist) puts up the resources while the working man puts up the labor. A normal sharing of this pot is 50/50. Good luck with those numbers in the macro economy.

The opposing viewpoint says that, generally, capitalists and laborers get wealthier, or poorer, together. When they don't, something is wrong. So, you bet your bippy there is something wrong today. And these are the capitalists (Republican) words. Crony capitalists have all the connections and all the power to twist things their way, keep the working man down and stifle competition.

The result has been wages more or less unchanged since 1968.

Comments

It looks as though the level of poor people, or those who need some sort of help, is moving up into the middle class. Average people are losing their jobs or are having their wages decreased, but at the same time prices are going up for food, energy, health care, and education—everything. That's not a good sign.

Truly part of the problem of the middle class contracting is that these words, such as inflation, deflation, etc., are just words to politicians, economists, and CEOs. Many of them don't have a clue and have never seen entire families homeless and with nothing to eat. Why is it that most of the Fed efforts tend to take from the poor and give to the rich? When do the poor finally realize it?

Former Labor Secretary Robert Reich once said: During periods when the very rich took home a larger proportion of income (like the Roaring 20s and

Depression, the country did poorly, and again since 1980), growth slowed, wages for the average person stagnated and we suffered giant downturns (Reich, 2011). Coincidence? Not likely. That income to the rich peaked in 1928 and 2007—the two years just preceding the biggest downturns (Reich). If true, then maybe there is a correlation between inequality and poor performance in an economy.

Women entering the work force has had repercussions, both good and bad. "In the 1960s only 12 percent of married women with young children were working for pay; by the late 1990s, 55 percent were." (Lerman & Schmidt, 1999) When that wasn't enough, people started going into debt. Someone forgot to tell people that just because their house value goes up is no reason to spend beyond their means. Once again, no one is willing to back off from their bloated and unearned lifestyle. On the bad side, having both adults work can't be good for home life, heaven forbid one of them has to work a late shift. It's not good for relationships and not good for the kids, who grow up estranged from both parents but love the babysitter. Obviously there was more money coming in for a while, not counting the cost of extra transportation, lunches, and babysitters.

Average Americans don't own stocks, except possibly in their IRAs and 401ks. They also, generally, except for the token quota allocation, don't go to

Harvard Business School. They went to community college if they were lucky and still have plenty of debt.

It's an uphill struggle against an increasingly stacked deck. It will be tough to circumvent because Washington caters to the wealthy.

So much for the trickle-down theory, or the notion that a rising tide lifts all boats.

For the first time in decades, most United States citizens have received no benefits from the economic growth in this nation. The growing influence of corporate lobbyists has perverted the system of government. The media, which is now just another corporate conglomerate that benefits from the same graft and corruption as the other corporations, has been bought by the rich. Who would have thought it?

Washington is either clueless or mystified or corrupt beyond even my wildest dreams. Picture them having a drink and either laughing at us or kidding themselves into believing all is well. Actually, for them all is well. But, what goes around comes around. You reap what you sow. At least I hope that's the case.

From an inequality of income standpoint, do you realize that all of the Fed money printing did nothing for the average citizen? All it did was make the rich richer, from the bankers to the corporations, both of which are richer now than ever. Right there at the trough also is Wall Street with business as usual. No one went to prison from the 2008 debacle. At least they went to prison during the Enron/World Com/Adelphi/Tyco scandals. Nothing was accomplished and nobody cares. How long can this go on? There must be some guideline from the past to tell us how long we must complain before we get fed up and revolt.   When I grow up I want to be Big Oil, Big Pharma, Big Banks, or Wall Street.

Although a politician is a politician regardless of whether a Democrat or a Republican, neither is out to help you. In some cases, they're just plain evil. In a cock fight I would still have to give the Republicans the edge. Their pandering to big business is embarrassing as well as a stated mandate in their platform. They don't even try to hide it. I don't know what to say about the Democrats. Their mandate is better, more for equality; but somehow when the smoke clears they can't help being scumbags also. I guess they just don't know any better.

"The United States is no longer a democracy, it's an oligopoly. A recent study by Princeton and Northwestern found that the lobbying special interests groups control everything while the average American citizen has no say in anything—and nobody in Washington cares" (Boren, 2014).

It's not that some leaders are not worth more, it's just how much more?
"Once seen as the land of opportunity, the United States today has rising inequality and a political system that benefits the rich at the expense of others, resulting

in lower growth and risking the death of the American dream," (Stiglitz, 2012).

"The American dream is now a myth, at least for those who have been here for generations. Stiglitz said, U.S. inequality is at the highest point in nearly a century and the gap between those with the median income and those at the top is growing. Today, a child's life chances are more dependent on the income of his or her parents than in Europe, or any other of the advanced industrial countries for which there are data " (Stiglitz, 2012). In 2012 Democrats felt that Mitt Romney was out of touch with the average person due to his wealth. Not a doubt in my mind.

"We are being conned into believing that we get the fast growth of the economy because of paying a few at the top huge amounts of money. Presumably the growth wouldn't happen if we didn't pay them. History doesn't bear that out. The U.S. economy grew faster in the decades after the Second World War, when inequalities were lower, than it did after 1980" (Stiglitz, 2012). "Even the textbooks today insinuate that there must be a trade-off between an egalitarian society and growth. Sooner or later, inequality starts to fester and ultimately causes social, economic, and political instability, which then leads to lower growth." Stiglitz (2012). Gee, a textbook that's incorrect. And they say Russia tries to change history. Shades of George Orwell.

"Countries with the highest degree of equality have the most prosperous economies, such as those in Scandinavia". (Stiglitz, 2012).

The fact that people like Warren Buffet espouse new rules for the rich paying more should tell you there is inequality, why else would he be saying anything? The suggested rule by the way only suggests that the rich merely pay the same percentage as the poor. It definitely indicates that the rich are currently not paying their fair share, or there would be no need to have the discussion.

The Republican proposals to extend the Bush-era tax cuts was just one more indication of the rich getting what they want and the Republican platform being either ill-informed or simply corrupt—or merely biased toward the rich—or plain evil! How many do not know that the Republican Party is the party of the rich and has been for over 100 years? So as not to be too biased, I have already dealt with the Democratic platform and the 800 pound gorilla drawing unemployment. Once again, that just goes to show you that you can fool most of the people most of the time. This logic seems so simple.

Although there are many examples of ridiculous pay to CEOs in the Appendix, here's just one to get the furious juices boiling: Chipotle paid its CEO, Steve Ells, $25.1 million in cash and stock in 2012. It paid Montgomery F. Moran, the company's other co-chief executive, $24.4 million. Mr. Ells, earned 778 times the median salary at the company in 2012, (Turner, 2014). Again, no one is saying that these guys are not doing a good job, or that the burritos don't taste great; but come on, how much is enough?

It's a poor and unwise pay structure that pays short term at the expense of long term value. Stock rights are similar to stock options, which give executives the right to buy shares in a company at a discount. But with stock appreciation rights, executives are granted blocks of shares when the company's stock price increases without ever having to exercise options. They don't even have to ever put any money up!

"Mr. Ells has received more than 600,000 Chipotle shares over the last four years and has sold more than 548,000 during that same time" (Turner, 2014). He's gone. Somehow the board has the cart before the horse. Because this guy is taking the money and running, the board thinks they need to give him some more as an incentive. Is that what Wharton and Harvard teach now? Hey, I blew all my money at the track, so give me some more and I might show up for work tomorrow.

So, to whom do you complain? The board? Same old same old. How do they get away with it without some accomplices unless they kept controlling interest?

"When the market tanked a few years ago, Walmart workers lost about 18% of the value of their 401ks. Yet Walmart's CEO saw gains of $2.3 million in his $47 million retirement plan" (Williams, 2011). How can that be fair? Shouldn't they be feeding from the same trough?

Why do we put up with it? Hey, I just got a cool new game on my phone! And they now have an app for my reality TV show. Does that answer your question?

Speaking of either harebrained or merely corrupt ideas, whose idea was it to repeal the Glass Steagall Act? This was the act passed into law back in the 1930s to separate Commercial (those who lend money) banks from Investment (those who generally raise money in investment form) banks. After all, things were getting out of hand in the 1920s, and the banks were doing their fair share of messing up. Wasn't the effort in 1933 to control speculative banks? I guess it must have been, otherwise the bank lobbyists wouldn't have been whining all those years to repeal it. How in the world did they ever sucker Bill Clinton in 1992, a brilliant man and a Democrat, into repealing it? Did we somehow improve as a species since then? If not, why in the world would you repeal it? Now the powers that be have changed the Net Capital Rule which increasing the debt ratios from about 12 times their assets to a ratio of 33 to 1. The problem with that is that if the market goes against them and their investment goes down 3% they are bankrupt.

I hold out no hope that a politician gives a rats whether the elderly can pay their mortgage and eat. That would be too much to ask. But a strong economist should, and probably has, observed that because the elderly are broke; they must continue to work, taking those jobs from the young. The youth unemployment rate is somewhere around 25% so how come they are not burning cars and rampaging through cities?

Assume for a moment that democracy is the opposite of capitalism as some would have you believe. Democracy gives everyone a say while capitalism rewards those who take risks, innovate, or have capital. That's is much too simple. Capitalism as practiced in the United States gives rewards to cronies-the only ones with any capital, and therefore the ability to take risks.

History says that, as opposed to the "Trickle Down theory", which said that if you give all the money to the rich, some of it will rub off on the poor, or the rich will somehow spend it and therefore care for the others. Left to their own devices the rich will not take care of the others. Intervention and some guidance is necessary.

Quantitative easing and endless bailouts only help the capitalists and the more affluent, and are not solutions to an economic downturn. They only create greater bubbles, income inequality, and create an even bigger crisis later.

Some say the rich will be hurt more because they have farther to fall. I believe that's as it should be because the middle and lower classes have already hit rock bottom. They have nothing left to lose. Gee, does that make it OK because we are already at rock bottom? Doesn't that corroborate that the rich have too much?

Rumor has it that corporations need to rid themselves of employees because meanie Uncle Sam is making them comply with too tough regulations like Obamacare. Poor babies. If things were anymore skewed toward the rich and the corporate hierarchy they would be sleeping in the same bed.

More BS from the whiners. Mitt Romney wanted to de-fund PBS. Yeah, that three dollars will help balance the books. Besides, table scraps for the likes of him.

We don't reward the brightest and best. We reward connections and family wealth. Even if we did it's still unseemly.

Everything we as a country stand for goes against the super-rich situation. If you believe in Democracy, or a Republic or whatever you want to call us, you should be very concerned.

Here's another of the dull platitudes from the wealthy: inequality of outcomes doesn't matter as long as there is equality of opportunity. Who comes up with these? Let's face it, with all that insulated, interwoven network, how in the world could any outsider- think normal, average person, get ahead? Then there's the one about "incredibly high incomes reflect comparably incredible contributions to the economy." Right. They contributed most of the heartache and financial woes associated with the 2008 debacle; then taxpayers had to bail them out.

Getting a college degree is no longer a guarantee of financial security either. Their jobs have been farmed out overseas in order to save money for the rich. So they work at McDonalds. The cost of education is outrageous due to the government stepping in to pay for education, allowing the universities to go wild with fee increases. Some of the universities are probably four times as expensive as they should be. Who cares, if you're not paying for it? But you are.

We Don't Even Care!

Have we given up? Not that I blame us, but we all know that the weasels love it when we do that. Is it because we feel that there is no use? The system is rigged and we can't get around it? Will it take blood in the streets? Or is it simply because we are too busy wanting something for nothing, we like the system that cares for us? Or, because of both family members having to work, we really just do not have time? This is our fault, whoever us is. I know it's not easy because these guys have all the cards, but gee guys, we should do something. In the past, at least, after a while, the peasants would rise up and revolt, a war broke out or someone got their head chopped off. So be it. Someone has to watch the store. Like letting a fox guard the hen house. Given the opportunity, we all do bad things and human nature is basically selfish and self-preserving. Self-policing is a joke. You have got to be diligent and vigilant. Give them an inch and they will take a mile. Some of us still believe just because the rich dribble out a pittance just to keep us in line that they will continue to care for us on some reasonable basis. What baloney. These guys would kill their mothers for a nickel. We are so busy watching reality TV and the football game? Can't miss them, can we? Due to texting on our iPhones we hardly notice the deterioration.

Starbucks

You want to know what's wrong with your country? I guess this could also be thought of as a marketing testimonial. I've got to take my hat off to them. Stop in Starbucks sometime. Talk about a tragedy on so many levels. Who would have ever thought people would pay $4 for a cup of coffee?

. Clearly a capitalistic triumph. Starbucks doesn't sell coffee. They sell a gaudy, 20-ounce coffee-based creation, with whipped cream and syrup, served in throwaway plastic cups. Lots more profit. Check out their executive stock-option grant. Remember Zoo zoo's petals? Instead of an angel getting their wings, every time a cash register rings, a CEO gets rich. Every time an executive gets a grant, the shareholders get less. These options are buried in the fine print of the SEC filings, are not therefore, deducted from earnings and so profitability is overstated. And it isn't a little thing. It's a zero sum game, folks. This is our wake-up call. When you sit around Starbucks banging away at your iPhone, you have given up many of your rights to complain about inequality.

Nothing Is Fair

Nothing is fair, nothing has ever been fair, and nothing is ever going to be fair until human nature changes. So I guess you have to put in place social mores that say it is good to be fair. *Brave Heart* wasn't Mel Gibson. William Wallace (BraveHeart) was around 6'6" when everyone else was 5'6," so he ruled by sheer strength as a bully. Which is great if you're William Wallace; not so great if you are just a hardworking, kind, 5'6" worker-bee. Granted, CEOs don't necessarily have to be big physically anymore, but the traits of aggression are the same. All Louis XV had to do was give out a little bread—but the rich are always greedy beyond reasonableness. Alexander the Great, Genghis Khan, Napoleon, etc.—all just aggressive—why do we fawn over them so much? Is a conqueror really so good?

It does appear that in India and China, adopting liberal economies with a profit motive is working, but, welcoming creative destruction? Come on! Not likely. She goes on to tie most other improvements of late, like wider spread democracy, the liberation of women, improved life expectancy, increased levels of education, spiritual growth, and artistic explosion to the same thing—capitalism. Sheer speculation!

"Ask any CEO, and they will tell you capitalism and business get a bum rap in the insinuation that they only act out of self-interest, being selfish and greedy and exploitative" (French, 2014) They would say that, wouldn't they?

Anti-capitalists insist it has been FDR's New Deal, the Tennessee Valley Authority (TVA) and the Federal Deposit Insurance Corporation (FDIC), to name just a few government programs that have created the dandy living we enjoy. There may or may not be some truth to that. However, while these folks want to blame dog-eat-dog cowboy capitalism for the crash of 2007–09 (The very fact that they use those terms should make you suspicious of their theories), it was, in fact, directly a result of Roosevelt's creation of depression-era pro-housing government programs like the FHA, Fannie Mae, Freddie Mac, and deposit insurance, that allowed banks to be absolved of responsibility. No doubt there is some truth in this also. It sure is easy to throw stones. As I explained in the Depression Era section, even though his heart was in the right place, there were flaws in New Deal spending.

Where would the money come from to wander around the planet fighting wars? Pity the poor Republican. It was Obama (not saying I'm a fan) who said "capitalism didn't work when it was tried in the 1920s; it didn't lead to the postwar booms of the 50s and 60s, and it didn't work during the last decade" (French, 2014).

I cannot disagree that big government is a culprit when it comes to debasing the currency through money printing as evidenced by the fact that the currency is worth a fraction of what it once was. Remember, as it applies to Inequality, inflation helps the rich.

Can Equality Exist in Capitalism?

For some, maybe. If a business doesn't earn a profit, it goes broke. So, if the automakers don't earn any money, they go out of business, right? Then, new more lean businesses start up to do their job better. Oh wait, that didn't happen, did it? Oops. So much for capitalism and the freedom to fail. Back to crony-capitalism where it's who you know or who you can bribe; who has the money and lots of regulatory hoops to jump through (which only the rich and connected know how to jump through). How can capitalists ask for a handout? So I guess capitalism works just fine for the rich CEOs. In addition to crony capitalism we now have casino capitalism, instant and easy gratification that translates to a good quarterly report. Quarterly Reports equal the attention span of all investment bankers. If that were not true how come that's all they talk about on the financial news? Forget about hard work, real investment in production, and innovation. Usually those traits manifest themselves in long term thinking, planning and profits.

CEO's and other cheaters and greedy rich people have learned to play the system for their own benefit and get better at it. Perhaps that's why Democracies have an evolutionary cycle. People want more and more, Real capitalists have control. Just remember that when you turn over your savings to some mutual fund manager. Don't forget for a minute that labor and their unions want their pound of flesh also. Big health benefits and bulging pension plans. All the investors want is for the stock to rise. And back to the top executives for their last bite of the apple—a golden parachute. After a very short time as CEO of Time Warner, Robert Marcus negotiated the sale of the company. Mr. Marcus received a golden parachute worth $80 million for no longer working, and after a short time at the controls (Johnson R. , 2014). Our fault, yours and mine, for letting them get away with this. If you think he is an isolated example, you need to get up and change the channel! A couple of reminders. These guys take no risk, especially with their own money, and seriously, do you really think anyone is worth that kind of pay? Even Steve Jobs. All he did was come up with a toy—a phone! You'd think he invented fire. Are the rich harder working and smarter? Well, maybe a little. But we should be talking percentages of difference here, not factors of 400! No wonder we can't make good cars. Nobody has their eye on that ball, too busy with their own little greed trip.

Capitalism is not self-sufficient. To sustain itself, capitalism requires constant expansion and exploitation of new markets. Capitalism must constantly be fed new markets to devour. That may explain a lot about why we constantly hear how we must expand. Since some natural resources are finite, the rich and connected are constantly looking for new emerging markets. They encumber the emerging nation with debt in return for funding development projects. When these emerging nations are unable to repay, an agency like the International Monetary Fund or the World Bank, who is a friend of the rich and big business, impose "structural readjustment" programs usually favoring western banks, take away control of the natural resources, and depress incomes of the local population.

This is what the Greeks are whining about, although in their case, it may be a stretch. It (IMF, Capitalism etc) all has to do with how initially good ideas turn out to be a tool of the rich and powerful.

Save money? Invest for the long term? Not a chance. Silly boy. Who are we kidding? These are not the ideas of Ayn Rand and the CEOs. I don't think there an app for this on the IPhone.

Is there a place for morality in Capitalism?

What ever happened to the golden rule? Or doesn't that apply to business? Generally, if you follow the golden rule, you are doing the right thing. My guess is there is no mention of such a rule in any business mandate or policy manual. Or is there some sense nowadays that morality doesn't matter anymore? Just take a moment and think of those times when someone cuts in line ahead of you, or is unjustly mean to you, or lies to you either personally or in a business environment. If you think that's wrong, then you are saying you believe in morality. So it matters. It matters because in order for those CEO's to take home such huge bonuses someone else will suffer. Corporate capitalism is still a zero-sum game. For someone to win, someone else has to lose.

To say that government is a group of humans that rules over other humans is a bit too strong, even if it's true.

Not that there shouldn't be a discussion about any government being evil incarnate. Even if big government is corrupt it was likely not deliberately set up that way. That means if we don't do what they tell us, they will punish us (hurt us). Either physically or financially. These believers also say, "The people who are the government take from those others. Again, no one is disputing that we are taxed. But let's be fair, a lot of that money is slated for projects to help the average citizen. Notwithstanding the war machine, what about roads, bridges, welfare support systems (yes, it could stand a going over), education, health care, etc. When someone comes down like this on government they weaken their otherwise winning hand. You're beating up on someone for the wrong reason

Is it moral for one group of men to take money by force from everyone else? No one likes having their money taken away so, taking money by force certainly should be immoral.

Many people say that letting the market and entrepreneurs have their way leads to wealth inequality. There will be people who are poor and people who end up rich, and that's immoral (they claim). A wee bit of a problem here is the use of the word immoral. How about just not fair? And don't you want to live in a fair civilization?

Most people agree that capitalism is stunningly successful at creating wealth, but it is immoral because it puts the importance of profit and wealth accumulation before the interests and human rights of people, namely the laboring class. Capitalism is working as it is supposed to: creating as much wealth as humanly possible. Hooray for capitalism. Free market economists and politicians say that it makes everybody's lives better. That is extremely debatable. If lives are not any better, then why bother to create all that wealth? Or, as I suspect, is the wealth not being distributed equally? We need to examine the playbook again to see exactly what is the purpose of civilization?

Kindness

Why wouldn't we adhere to the Samurai philosophy? It's filled with admirable traits. Honor being high on the list. Not that it doesn't go to extremes regarding war being somehow glorious and how really neat it is to die in battle. Actually it sucks to die in battle. I still admire the Japanese sense of honor- even if carried to extremes with the committing.

Human kindness has never weakened the stamina or softened the fiber of a free people. A nation does not have to be cruel to be tough. -Franklin D. Roosevelt. Change tough to strong and apply to individuals also. Have we discussed the folly of mistaking kindness and politeness for weakness?

By the way, making one wait in a doctor's office is a great example of shear rudeness. There just isn't any excuse- except they are greedy and trying to squeeze in all the billable hours then can. As for those lower down the food chain such as plumbers, electricians, mechanics etc., the excuse is even more unacceptable. As for the money part, I just spoke with a very good friend who just had a fuel pump replaced in his little truck. They charged him $675. I saw the part on line for anywhere from $40-$80. Labor in these parts for a back yard non dealer mechanic ranges from $65 to $75, although that is even too much. It's a two hour job max. So the mechanic cheated him by overcharging him $675 for a $230 job. That pretty stiff. That's just one example of a gazillion. I guess help thy neighbor is out the window. What about plain old decency?

Solutions

It is puzzling as to why more hasn't been done in the last 40 years to help the middle class. We could have simply addressed the problems, improved education, and done a better job of creating energy efficiency. Certainly someone should be assigned to figure out the health care situation. Why do we spend more than twice as much as anyone else yet our level of care is far worse than dozens of countries?

Everyone constantly heaps accolades on Adam Smith and treat his book, "The Wealth of Nations", written in 1776, as a bible for free market economic thinking. Mr. Smith is known as the Father of Economics and is best known for his theory of the "Invisible Hand." It basically means that leave the markets alone to do their thing and natural forces will see that all's well regarding income distribution and productions. Yeah, right. Ironic that a free market advocate was all for a progressive tax. With that in mind, why not try some of these on for size?

Let's establish a reasonable cut off for taxing. Say, after 250k in earnings, tax it at 60–70%. Same for small businesses.

Take the $10 million average income of almost ten years ago, forget about the 30 million average of 2014. Give them $1,000,000, which is 3 times what they are worth, and spread the remaining $9 million dollars over 9 thousand employees at a $1,000 bonus. I'll bet that will increase productivity. Or, why not donate the $9 million to charity to feed 9,000 people for 10–20 weeks (5 months!)?

As to the minimum wage; say we increase it $1 an hour or $2,000 per year. A raise of a dollar for 5 employees would only cost about $10,000. Hummm. Let's see, as a small businessman/woman (according to government standards that could mean with a company of 500 employees!), the CEO is probably making at least $500,000. Take away $10,000 to make five families whole again and poor baby only has $490,000 left to squeak by. Get the point. Then maybe the price of McMansions would go back down to just ridiculous.

Instead of whining about the minimum wage, why not address the real problem, the wage gap and obscene pay for the top executives? The minimum wage discussion would go away if those greedy misfits would take a reasonable pay. Is it proportional? Of course not. But think in terms of the reverse of the Walmart syndrome—a few pennies less on some items doesn't make up for many people not having any job. So you would be willing to pay a little more for a hamburger if you were making $10 per hour. You are already paying double for gas, and you are managing to buy it! So, a few pennies more in the pockets of the poor will not break the backs of the rich.

Equally as important, and extremely difficult; we need to go back several years to claw back money from CEOs, Wall Street, sports figures, and entertainers—retrieving 75% of bonuses and payments. Who in the world is going to allow that to happen, you ask. Well, no one, of course, without some force behind it. Let's face it, there is going to have to be some real pain here for us to get back on our feet.

Which reminds me, as to the idea that all the rich "producers" will migrate elsewhere. Fine. Just check your money at the door. This country was settled by religious fanatics (although hard working), adventurer/ explorers (again, hardy, but maybe not the most desirable dinner guests), and criminals (in the case of Georgia). Yet we somehow managed to thrive. Do you really think we can't start over without these guys?

Actually, the financial industry should be systematically annihilated. No kidding, the world would be a better place without these people. They don't create anything! They just scrape the cream off the top after moving money around. On the surface, that would be a good thing, moving money from where it is not needed to where it is needed. Except that is not what they do. It doesn't matter whether the money is needed or not—just move it around and get a commission.

Wealth Tax

Perhaps on a bit less draconian level, there is actually a glimmer of hope, especially outside of the United States. Some economic players have actually seen the light, recognize the problems facing the world fiscally, and are looking for ways to correct it.

Households all over the developed world may soon face a global wealth tax. Cyprus and the government's confiscation of money may have been a wake-up call. The idea, like all ideas, is gathering steam as the White House, New York Mayor Bill de Blasio, the International Monetary Fund, individuals such as Warren Buffett, billionaire investor Bill Gross and many others all climb on board. Gross centers his reasoning on why capital should be taxed differently than labor. Good question, especially when the rich have most of the capital and the poor provide most of the labor. That clearly makes it a preferential law for the rich. You can understand the logic, even if you don't agree with the reason for it, which is that advanced economies are deeply in debt.

Some of the advanced economies such as England, Ireland, and Spain have increased the top tax rate on high income earners a bit over the last five or six years. The United States continues to lead the world in hubris with a tiny 3.5% increase, and even that with plenty of loopholes.   The good news is that the IMF is on the job and looking to do some good. According to what they call their revenue-maximizing rate (mostly for the main Organization of Economic Cooperation and Development countries) they are trying to head for a 60% tax level (Mitchell, 2014). Good for them.

Let me digress with an example. It works the same as our war policy. First, we say we want nothing to do with the particular skirmish. Next we say we will only send in a few advisers. Then we increase the advisers to a few thousand. When that doesn't work, we say we will do a few air strikes but no boots on the ground. Follow that up with a few troops to "support" the locals. Finally, the locals can't do the job so we will have to, so we will systematically start sending in troops, increasing them as needed according to the wishes of the military industrial **complex. I** just had to get that in, even if it didn't apply (which it does). Look for the rhetoric to begin because indebted governments are in need and will look to get the money anywhere they can, like a big one-time levy on capital assets. Whether it is kosher or not is up for discussion.

Bear in mind when you hear the rich whine that 70% was the rate in effect just prior to the Reagan tax cuts. Did we discuss that Reagan was a charmer, a movie star? Gee, I wonder why we're in such deep trouble all the time. To pat the IMF on the back again, it appears they are much more willing to care less about the rich and their petty gripes from the back seat of the Rolls.

There is no question that taxing the rich is the right thing to do. Furthermore, I don't care about all the pontificating and huffing and puffing done by the rich and the Republicans. What I have trouble with is determining why what I know to be correct doesn't always work. Maybe it needs some tweaking. In France, President François Hollande passed a 75% tax on income above one million euros yet there is evidence he is having trouble pulling the economy out of the doldrums (Ruitenberg, 2013).

Those who are outraged over the compensation of CEOs want government intervention and a shift in focus from a company's shareholders and board to its employees. Yea! The age old story about who is important and who really represents the company. Good luck with that argument, even if correct. It is an uphill battle with
Road-blocks.

No one is saying that these measures would make everything perfect. More than anything, it would show some fairness in life and, therefore, maybe the middle classes would have a chance, feel better about themselves, and be willing to go the extra mile toward some corrective action. Obviously there are many other things to be done to cure the problems, not the least of which would be to stop spending money like madmen.

Here's a thought. Every time some CEO bets the farm, make sure it's his farm!

APPENDIX A - TYPES OF HUMANS

Speculative Estimates Only

Just Evil and kill for pleasure	10%
Amoral – will use and ruin you	30%
Pretty people	10%
Average People – Have been dealt a bad	40%

or unfair hand. But still only human, selfish, self-serving, survivalists, who will level the playing field if they get a chance.

The Decent Ones	10%

No wonder things are going so poorly.

There's nothing scarier than a self-righteous fanatic. Not only is it tough to stop but also it's easy to be swayed; just like we are swayed by aggression. Think about that the next time you are fascinated by the bad boy or girl. There isn't going to be any wake up on Christmas morning for Scrooge with a change of heart, saying "God bless us everyone."

APPENDIX B - HOW THE RICH GOT RICH

Speculative Estimates Only

Worked hard for it	15%
Inherited it	15%
Right Place, Right Time	15%
Lucky, overpaid inventors	15%
Pushy, Mean, Amoral, Selfish	15%
Drawing Undeserved Disability	15%
Athletes, Actors, Musicians	10%

APPENDIX C - WEALTH DISTRIBUTION

Speculative Estimate Only

Percent	Income ($)	Number of People	Total
.01	35,000,000	1	$35,000,000
.04	10,000,000	4	$40,000,000
.05	5,000,000	5	$25,000,000
.4	1,000,000	40	$40,000,000
.5	350,000	50	$17,500,000
9	100,000	900	$90,000,000
90	35,000	9000	$315,000,000

| Average | $562,500,000/10,000 – | | $56,250 |

APPENDIX D - EXAMPLES OF OVERKILL

Richard Fuld, Lehman Brother's head liar, was paid $500 million over an eight-year period (Ross & Gomstyn, 2008). Lehman Brother no longer exists so that ought to tell you how the company did during the same time frame.

Lloyd Blankfein, the CEO of Goldman "only" took $600,000 one year and made a big deal of it. But he received $68 million the previous year--a year that saw the investments of millions destroyed (Pizzigatti, 2011)!

The New York Times reported that Home Depot's share price had fallen 12% over the previous five years, while its rival, Lowes, had gone up 173%. Did the board even slap the CEO's hands? Nah. Instead of sending Robert Nardelli back to the paint department, his buddies on the compensation committee decided he deserved to earn almost a quarter of a billion dollars over that five-year stretch. Wait! It gets better. Nardelli got a severance package reported to be $210 million (Clothier, 2007). This guy did nothing right!

Dennis Kozlowski, the CEO of Tyco International was a narcissistic, egomaniac espousing a "can do" management style-that's business speak for aggressive, mean and greedy. He exemplified bravado, condescension for others, and ostentatious misuse of stolen funds ($6,000 shower curtain, a $17 million apartment, and $2 million dollar birthday parties). Of course, the press loved him (you know, women loved him and men wanted to be him), while his competitors and critics were afraid of him. Pathetic. He was a selfish, predatory jerk. He's the kind of guy who takes pleasure in destroying others. It's hard for normal people to believe that behind that smirk on the face of certain people there is nothing but meanness looking for an opportunity to stick it to you or make you look bad. At least Kozlowski went to prison (Gorman, 2013).

In 2003, General Motors' Rick Wagoner got a pay hike to $2.2 million, while guiding the company to its biggest loss in a decade (Bonner & Rajiva, 2007). And the money just keeps on rolling in, says Evita.

Lee Raymond, retiring CEO of ExxonMobil Corporation got $400 million dollars as he sauntered out the door. U.S. Senator Byron Dorgan (D-ND) called that a shameful display of greed while consumers were having to pay $3.00 per gallon several year back. Just like inflation, stick around and things will get worse. Dorgan even suggested a windfall profits tax on oil companies. Good luck with that. Exxon reported the highest profit in the history of corporate America in 2005 (Romero & Holusa, 2006). Today we read that while farmers struggle to pay the fuel bills (let's not feel too much sorrow for the farmers) and drivers are paying painful prices to fill their gas tanks (regardless of the oil prices), the oil companies are rolling in cash and their retired executives are getting obscene retirement benefits.

"These oil companies are particularly heinous considering they control the fate of most of us in the United States. No doubt there is plenty of blame to go around, but the price of oil is clearly a big factor in reducing our standard of living. The expense of oil is in so much of our production, through fertilizers, cars, plastics, etc. Price gouging and market manipulation is the norm in this industry, and is working to serve the forces of individual greed and corporate gluttony at the painful expense of millions of American consumers" (Dorgon, 2007). Everyone I know in the business makes $150,000. How come when oil prices were at $40 per barrel, oil companies were reporting then-all-time record profits yet the prices are doubled or tripled now, so I doubt you can count high enough to determine the true profit picture and pay scales. This is an industry gone wild-at the public's expense. From an investment standpoint one would have to ask why they didn't bank some of that windfall profit for a rainy day or increase energy supplies, instead of paying themselves fat wages.

Michael Dell took home $153 million in 2006 by exercising options during a time when the company seriously was in trouble. The prior year former CEO Kevin Rollins netted $39 million. The two received over $281 million in that five-year span while the company stock, according to Hodgson's report, slipped 1.7% in that same five-year time frame, compared with 43% gains for the S&P 500. Rollins' total excludes options gains realized when he was president and chief operating officer, like the $36 million he got in the 12 months leading up to July 2004, when he became CEO (Harkinson, 2011). That's a lot of money for a company that appears to be getting worse. It must be nice to be a boy genius and reap bennies for years at the expense of your employees.

Alan Mulally took the Ford Motor CEO reins in 2006. Over his first three years, Ford lost $30 billion. Over the next two, Ford gained back less than $9.3 billion, yet they are celebrating in the street like they did something wonderful. Meanwhile Mulally got $56 million in stock and $26.5 million in annual pay in 2010. That's 910 times the pay of entry-level Ford workers who have been making $14 an hour since 2007. Must be nice. Here, as in so many examples, there is a common methodology. Fire people and shrink the company to profits. Mulally got $19.5 million just for signing on. Ford stock declined 41% during that five years. Ford's response was the old, "We had to pay him that much to get him away from

Boeing." They should have fired him from both Boeing and Ford (Pizzigatti, 2011).

AT&T CEO Edward Whitacre, Jr., got $57.3 million in 2003–05 in salary, bonuses, options, long-term incentive pay, restricted stock grants, and other pay. He earned $85 million during a five-year period, an average of about $17 million a year, according to a report from the Corporate Library called "Pay for Failure: The Compensation Committee Is Responsible ." Whitacre will continue as a consultant for three years after he retires—at more than $1 million a year. He'll also receive lifetime access to a corporate jet, a car, an office, and a support staff. He's in line for an annual pension of $5.3 million, as well (Payne, 2011). I don't care if he invented chocolate and popcorn, he's paid way too much. Besides, AT&T was going broke before Cingular did a reverse merger on them. Long-term shareholders, have been big losers under Whitacre's stewardship. Although AT&T stock did advance some after the mergers, it still did poorly over the long run especially compared to the Standard & Poor's 500 Index fund over the same period. And this was in 2005, before the crash (Payne) AT&T makes a habit of over-rewarding their stars. They did it before with Robert Allen who received $16 million while cutting 50,000 jobs in 1995" (Payne).

"EMC Corp. CEO Joseph Tucci received $57.3 million in 2003–05 in salary, bonuses, restricted stock, options, and other compensation, according to company documents. Shareholders, meanwhile, have gotten the shaft. Shares of the data-storage developer have under-performed sharply in the past five years, losing 18%" (Brush, 2006).

"CEO Samuel Palmisano of the IBM Corp received $65.5 million in salary, bonuses, restricted stock, options, long-term incentive pay, and other compensation in 2003–05 (Brush, 2007). He also has a pension that will pay at least $1.2 million a year. Shareholders have not done nearly as well. They are up 19% in the same 12 months, but over that five-year period, they were down about 18%" (Hiltzik, 2015). Tom Watson would be another one rolling over in his grave.

Al "Chainsaw" Dunlap is right up there with Genghis Khan and Attila the Hun. "He didn't attend his own parents' funerals. He allegedly threatened his first wife with guns and knives. She charged that he left her with no food and no access to their money while he was away for days. His divorce was granted on grounds of extreme cruelty. That's the characteristic that endeared him to Wall Street, which applauded when he fired 11,000 workers at Scott Paper, then another 6,000 (half the labor force) at Sunbeam... His plant closings kept up his reputation for ruthlessness but made no sense economically, and Sunbeam's financial gains were really the result of Dunlap's alleged book cooking" (Fastenburg, 2010)

"Cendant CEO Henry Silverman provides an obscene example. On top of his $54.4 million in 2003 pay, he has more than $287 million in stock options not yet cashed in. In retirement, he'll get a lavish pension and perks such as use of company cars and aircraft. When he dies, his heirs will be able to buy his company paid for with a $100 million life insurance policy provided by the company shareholders" (Sklar, 2004).

Why are workers and shareholders earning less or being downsized so the offspring of the CEOs don't have to work for 1000 years?

Colgate-Palmolive's Reuben Mark was the highest paid CEO in 2003 with compensation totaling $141.1 million. He was also on Business Week's list of CEOs who gave shareholders the least for their pay; shareholder return for 2001–2003 was a negative 19 percent (Sklar).

"The poster child for mad cash disease was Disney CEO Michael Eisner. His compensation averaged $121.2 million a year over a six-year period, reports *Forbes*, while Disney shareholders had an annualized total return (including dividends) of negative 5 percent. Eisner's average yearly pay was 3,796 times as much as the average worker's and 300 times as much as the U.S. President's" (Sklar, 2004). There seems to be a pattern at Disney, because just as you were recovering (partially) from shock, along comes Robert Iger after Eisner. Iger served (himself mostly, it would seem) from 2005 thru today. Some of his paydays include $28 million in 2011, 34 million in 2013 and 43 million in 2014 (Sklar).

For the sake of political correctness and equal rights, no list would be complete without Leona Helmsley. She was known as the Queen of Mean. Helmsley left no small detail overlooked, was a perfectionist and had little patience. She was known for surprise inspections and harsh criticism. She once said, "If something is wrong, the first time, I ask them to change it. The second time, I ask an octave higher. The third time, I ask the person if they want me to do it. The fourth time, if things aren't absolutely right, they're fired" (Romero F. , 2010). If you believe she ever gave anyone 4 chances, I've got a bridge to sell you.

One more for the ladies. Marge Schott pretty much offended everyone with whom she ever spoke. Schott was the CEO and president of the Cincinnati Reds from 1984 to 1999. I wonder how she got that position. "She repeatedly made slurs against African Americans, homosexuals and Asians. And she did it to her own team players" (Gibson, 2010). When an umpire had a heart attack and died during a game in 1996, she said "Snow this morning and now this. I don't believe it. I feel cheated" (Gibson).

This is just the tip of the iceberg. I leave it to the reader to determine if these are just normal humans with opportunity.

It seems like the bigger you are as a corporation (and an individual), the better you get at not paying tax on it. Not only do they not pay any tax but they very often get a rebate, making for an effective negative rate. Can you picture the greedy, lugging a bag of money almost too heavy to carry to the bank all the while whining that taxes are still too high (for them) and we should stop minimum wage and eliminate social security. What a picture. Huge compensation, don't even pay the tax on that huge paycheck, and then complain that the poor have it too good.

Time and time again we hear that they are only doing what is legal. If that is so, then the laws are unjust. Who do you think, through lobbying and campaign contributions, is making those laws?

Whether the government could use that money wisely to reduce the deficit and improve infrastructure is debatable since they are just as guilty of poor judgment and corruption. It would be an interesting study to see whether government flunkies are in bed with the corporate crooks or simply afraid of them. But there is no doubt that those on the low end of the income stream (minimum wage recipients) are getting screwed by these greasy skumbags.

Sacrifice is always for the other guy, not for them.

Just so we all know nothing has changed, no improvements have been made and certainly no one has learned any lessons, here are some updates on the corporation side:

From 2008 to 2012, Corning made $3.4 billion in profits and actually got a tax refund of $10 million, a negative tax rate. They avoided paying 4 billion in taxes. (Yaccato, 2015)

Merck got money back despite the fact that its income before taxes was $1.9 billion during the second quarter of 2013. They have been caught and charged with tax evasion before, from 1993 to 2001. (Yaccato, 2015) I believe we have touched upon the silly practice of fining these felons a far lesser amount than they avoided in taxes. If that's not temptation, I don't know what is. Like the auto manufacturer that calculates that it would be cheaper to let a certain number of people die in auto crashes than to fix the problem. Aren't they both amoral? Oh, and it took eight years to settle the case thanks to the corrupt and greedy legal system as well as the money Merck spent delaying it.

You would think they might have learned a lesson, although I don't know what that would be. Nope. By 2009 Merck was back in business (and not the pharmaceutical business). That year they got a $55 million refund on $5.7 billion in U.S. profits. In 2012,

Merck avoided paying $18.69 billion by putting $53.4 billion offshore. (Yaccato, 2015)

FedEx earned profits of $2.7 billion and got a $135 million tax refund from the IRS in 2011. They receive more than $1 billion a year from the U.S. Postal Service to provide air service for mail shipments. (Yaccato, 2015) Smart move Post Office, giving money to your competitors.

Walmart keeps $21.4 billion in profits offshore. They also participate in the rigged game called deducting executive pay by saying they are performance based.
The company employs 74 lobbyists and has spent $32.6 million lobbying to lower taxes even more over the past five years. (Yaccato, 2015)

Verizon is an example of yet another accounting miracle from a communications company. From 2008 to 2013, Verizon made over $42 billion in U.S. profits and got a tidy little tax refund of $732 million. Effective tax rate: minus 2%. In 2012, the company saved another $630 million in taxes by stashing $1.8 billion in offshore tax havens. (Yaccato, 2015)

Apple reportedly keeps $138 billion abroad, an amount which would generate $45 billion in taxes. Apple incorporated in Ireland and shifted billions of dollars in income from the U.S. The subsidiary they use for this scam had $30 billion on its books and no employees. (Yaccato, 2015)

Boeing made over $26.4 billion in U.S. profits from 2008-2013. At the standard corporate tax rate, it would have had a tax bill of just under $9 billion. Instead, it received a $401 million refund from the IRS, making their effective U.S. corporate income tax rate minus 2 percent. The company threatened to move its 777 passenger jet project out of Washington in 2013, inspiring the state government to cough up $8.7 billion in tax breaks. Boeing and the others love to tell the powers that be in Washington to stop spending so much money… just don't stop spending it on them. (Yaccato, 2015)

From 2010-12, Exxon paid less than half of the 35% rate they're supposed to pay, so in effect the company got a tax subsidy worth $6.2 billion. Exxon also had $43 billion in offshore profits, on which it paid no US tax at all. (Yaccato, 2015)

Pfizer made $43 billion from 2010 to 2012, and paid zero tax on that amount. Pfizer shifted the profits offshore to tax-free jurisdictions. They even got a couple of billion in federal tax refunds by transferring rights to a shell company in Liechtenstein. The company is said to have stashed as much as $73 billion in profits out of reach offshore. (Yaccato, 2015)

"GE has $110 billion stashed offshore, allegedly. This means avoiding $40 billion in taxes a year, enabling them to pay an effective tax rate of four percent – a ninth of the actual corporate tax rate. $33.9 billion in US profits between 2008 and 2013 resulted in a $3 billion refund from the IRS – an actual tax rate of minus 1%. As a thank you, the federal government gifted GE contracts worth $22 billion in taxpayers' money. In return, GE hired thousands of workers… In China and Mexico. CEO Jeffrey Immelt, who makes $19 million a year, has also advocated increasing taxes. On working families. Apparently corporate taxes are still too high." (Yaccato, 2015)

When talking about the top banks, the act of cheating the American people seems especially bad when the banks wouldn't exist if not for a gigantic bailout of $2.5 trillion taxpayer dollars. Citigroup was broke after the 2008 financial crisis, before Washington came to the rescue. After 5 years of lawyering they agreed to a $2.2 billion settlement to cover damages caused by the company's lending abuses.

Not only that but they were able to write off the cost of doing the illegal business. Citigroup made the taxpayer pay their legal bill. They paid zero tax in 2010 and had $42.6 billion in foreign profits parked offshore in 2012 on which it paid no US taxes. Another $11.5 billion down the drain. (Yaccato, 2015)

Microsoft is keeping $92.9 billion in profits off shore according to the Securities and Exchange

Commission. That's almost $30 billion in taxes the U.S. treasury are missing out on. (Yaccato, 2015)

"For sheer nerve, it's tough to beat the Bank of America. In 2012, the Bank had more than 300 separate subsidiaries incorporated in offshore tax havens. The Bank made $17.2 billion in profits that year. If that income were declared, they would have owed $4.3 billion in federal income tax. But by leaving those profits stashed in those tax-free havens, Bank of America paid zero tax to America. B of A was deeply involved in the mortgage crisis of 2008 that brought the global economy to the point of collapse. So, they gladly accepted a $1.3 trillion bailout from Washington. The Federal Reserve Board also gave the Bank amnesty from all legal claims and protection against losses from toxic mortgages up to $118 billion. It still made $4.4 billion in profits and somehow ended up with a $1.9 billion tax refund. At the same time, CEO Brian Moynihan (salary & benefits: $13.1 million) seems to think taxpayers' entitlements are too lavish. He endorsed calls to raise the eligibility age for Medicare to 70, and make significant cuts to Social Security." (Yaccato, 2015)

Any way you look at it these corporations are stiffing the US government and therefore taxpayers, plus eliminating jobs for United States workers.

GLOSSARY

Arbitrage: taking advantage of different prices in different places by buying in the cheap place and selling in the expensive place.

Austrian Business Cycle: Inflation sets off the business cycle. Austrian economists hold this to be the most damaging effect of inflation. According to Austrian theory, artificially low interest rates and the associated increase in the money supply lead to reckless speculative borrowing, resulting in clusters of mal-investments, which eventually have to be liquidated as they become unsustainable.

Bear Market: A downturn in the stock market of usually 20% or more over at least a two month period.

Boondoggle: Wasteful, expensive and pointless work, usually with someone else's money.

Bull Market: When the stock market seems to be on a never ending upward swing

Comparative Advantage: The ability of a party to produce a particular good or service at a lower margin and opportunity cost. Even if one country is more efficient in the production of all goods than another, both countries will still gain by trading with each other.

Consumer Price Index (CPI) is the broadest inflation measure published by U.S. Government, through the Bureau of Labor Statistics (BLS), Department of Labor:

Deflation: A decrease in the prices of goods and services, usually tied to a contraction of money in circulation.

Demonetize: To stop using, take from circulation, divest a currency of its value.

Depression: A recession where the peak-to-trough (highest to lowest point) contraction in real growth exceeds 10%.

Derivatives: An instrument (such as a future, option, or warrant) whose value derives from and is dependent on the value of an underlying asset.

Exchange rates: The value of one currency compared to another. It's how many dollars can be bought with another currency.

Fractional Reserve Banking: A system whereby banks can expand the money supply. Every time money is loaned out it gets redeposited somewhere else and can be relent- minus whatever reserve requirements are in place at the time. Assume a reserve requirement of 20%, which is high for simplicity. Starting with $100 in deposit at Bank A, that bank makes a loan of $80 and puts $20 in reserve. The person receiving the loan (borrower 1) buys something with the money and that recipient then puts the $80 in his bank. His bank (bank B) lends out 80% or $64 and places $16 in reserves. That borrower (2) pays for something and his seller takes the money to his bank. Bank C lends out $51.20 and places $12.80 in reserves. Borrower 3 pays for something and that recipient deposits the funds in his bank. His bank (bank D) lends $40.96 to borrower 4 who pays for something which gets deposited into the recipient's bank (E) who lends out $32.77 to borrower 5. That borrower paid someone for something and the recipient deposited the funds into his bank which lent out $26.22 putting the rest in reserves. So we started with, and still have, only $100- yet somehow there is $395.15 in use. Welcome to Fractional Banking. With a more realistic reserve of around 3 to 5% and continuing the lending the scam is exacerbated.

GDP (Goss Domestic Production): all the goods and services produced *by a nation*

Glossary

General Equilibrium Theory: Studies supply and demand fundamentals in an economy with multiple markets, with the objective of proving that a set of prices exists that will result in an overall equilibrium.
Great Depression: A depression where the peak-to-trough contraction in real growth exceeds 25%.

Hedonics: the product has been improved and that's why it's more expensive—so the price gets reduced back down and it is not inflation

Hyperinflation: An inflation rate at least in excess of four-digit annual percent change, where the involved currency becomes worthless, and people know it and don't want it. It is extremely rapid, or out of control, inflation. Hyperinflation is often associated with wars, economic depressions, and political or social upheavals. In both classical economics and monetarism, it is always the result of the monetary authority irresponsibly borrowing or printing money to pay all its expenses.

IMF -International Monetary Fund – a world lending organization

Inflation: a rise in the general level of prices so your currency buys fewer goods and services. Your money has less purchasing power (a loss of currency's value).

A different viewpoint is that the above is only the result of inflation. Inflation is strictly money printing, which causes a rise in the general level of prices. It is not the result, which includes increased prices and wages.

Inverted Yield Curve: When the difference in interest rates between the short and long terms narrows, the yield curve flattens. When long-term rates fall below short-term rates, you get the inverted yield curve. That means you have achieved the absurd condition where you are getting paid less money for loaning your money for a longer term, and at higher risk!

Labor Theory of Value: aka the cost-of-production theory of value, states that the value of an object is the cost to make it including labor, capital, land, or technology.

Marginal Theory of Value: (1870s) to have value an object must be both useful and scarce to a consumer as opposed to the Cost of Production Theory of Value believed by Classical Economists.

Glossary

Monetization of debt – printing new money as opposed to taxing or borrowing

Non-Accelerating Inflation Rate of Unemployment (NAIRU): A level of unemployment you can have without having inflation.

Quantitative Easing: A government monetary policy used to increase the money supply by buying government securities or other securities from the market. QE increases the money supply by flooding financial institutions with fiat capital (money created from thin air at the Federal Reserve), in an effort to promote increased lending and liquidity.

Quantity Theory of Money: When the supply of money goes up the price (value) comes down. Print money and value reduces.

Recession: Two or more consecutive quarters of contracting real (inflation-adjusted) GDP, where the downturn is not triggered by any unusual or "Black Swan event.

Sticky Prices: A theory that when unemployment rises, the worker's wages of those that were not let go do not fall accordingly.

The Velocity of Money: A larger number of transactions or faster movement of money (each piece of money is used more often), so it's like more money. Hyperinflation panics do this. It can be a vicious circle. The good news, if any, is it's a rare occurrence.

Too Big To Fail: An economic theory stating that certain banks (and other entities) are too intertwined in, and have too much effect on, the overall economy and therefore should get preferential treatment and not be allowed to fail because the result would be too much to bear for the economy.

Trickle Down Theory: The idea espoused by Arthur Laffer during the Reagan era, that, if you give money to the rich it will work its way down to the rest of us.

Glossary

REFERENCES

Altucher, J. (2015). *Hedge Funds Steal Money from Every Investment You Make.* BonnerandPartners.

Ames, M. (2012). *Exclusive: Failing Up with Dick Parsons.* www.thedailybanter.com.

Anderson, S., Cavanaugh, J., Collins, C., & Pizzigati, S. (2007). *Executive Excess 2007.* www.faireconomy.com.

Aquinas, S. T. (1265). *Summa Theologica.* www.Biography.com.

Baker, D. (2013). *Job Loss at $15 an Hour: Real Problem or Big Whopper.* www.cepr.com.

Berfield, S. (2012). *Versailles, Would be Biggest House in America.* Bloomberg.

Berrone, P. (2008). *) Global Compensation.* Routledge.

Blodget, H. (2011). *Finally, A Rich American Destroys The Fiction That Rich People Create The Jobs.* Daily Ticker.

Bonner, B. (2007b). *Excessive CEO Salaries Based on Confidence Rather Than Performance.* Agora Publishing.

Bonner, B. (2009). *It's the Water-slide into Hell! .* Agora Publishing.

Bonner, B., & Rajiva, L. (2007). *Mobs, Messiahs, and Markets: Surviving the Public Spectacle in Finance and Politics,.* John Riley and Sons.

Boren, Z. D. (2014). *Major Study Finds The US Is An Oligarchy.* www.Businessinsider.com.

References

Brat, D. (2014). *Dave Brat in Survey of 2014 House campaign websites.* www.ontheissues.org.

Brush, M. (2006). *CEOs who take the millions and run.* www.cordant.com.

Chung, D. (2015). *Individual Accountability for Corporate Wrongdoing.* Harvard Law School.

Clothier, M. (2007). *Home Depot's Nardelli Ousted After Six-Year Tenure.* Bloomberg.

CorpFlunky. (2014). *Top 1% share in World History.* Daily Kos.

Covert, B. (2013). *Here's How Fast Food Could Handle A $15 Minimum Wage Without Cutting Jobs.* www.Thinkprogress.org.

Crotty, j. (2009). *The Bonus-Driven "Rainmaker" Financial Firm: How These Firms Enrich Top Employees, Destroy Shareholder Value and Create Systemic Financial Instability .* www.peri.umass.edu.

DeSilver, D. (2013). *Suicides Account for Most Gun Deaths.* Pew Research.

Deutschman, A. (2005). *Is Your Boss a Psychopath?* www.fastcompany.com.

Dickinson, T. (2014). *The Biggest Tax Scam Ever.* www.rollingstone.com.

Dorgon, B. (2007). *Take This Job and Ship It: How Corporate Greed and Brain-Dead Politics Are Selling Out America.* St. Martin's Griffin.

Doyle, L. (2010). *JP Morgan's Perfect Quarter More Evidence "Game is Fixed".* www.Senseoncents.com.

Eder, S. (2009). *Study shows U.S. bank CEO pay dwarfs rest of world.* Reuters.

Epstein, V. (2005). *) U.S. Initial Jobless Claims Rise Last Week to 350,000 (Update2.* Bloomberg.

Fastenburg, D. (2010). *Top 10 Worst Bosses.* www.content.time.com.

Feloni, R. (2014). *The Reason CEO Pay Is So High Right Now Has Little To Do With Greed.* www.businessinsider.com.

Fournier, R. (2014). *How to Renounce America and Still Be Called a Patrio.* www.NationalLeader.com.

Frank, R. (2014). *Luxury CEO: The Poor Should Stop Whininh.* CNBC.com.

French, D. (2014). *Minimum Wage, Maximum Stupidity.* Casey Research.

French, D. (2014). *The Morality Test: Capitalism vs Government.* Casey Research.

Friedman, T. (2005). *It's a Flat World after All.* NYTimes.

Fry, E. (2005). *Pinstriped Psychopaths.* Daily Reckoning.

Fry, E. (2007). *Greed, Money, and Wall Street.* www.commodityonline.com.

Fry, E. (2007b). *Bonus Envy.* Agora Publishing.

Fry, E. (2010). *) The Truth Behind California's Pension Shortfall.* Daily Reckoning.

Germanos, A. (2015). *To Achieve Highly-Touted Development Goals, End Business-as-Usual,.* www.commondreams.org.

Gibson, M. (2010). *Top 10 Worst Bosses, Marge Schott.* www.content.time.com.

References

Gongloff, M. (2014). *Percentage Of Americans Living Below The Poverty Level, 1980-2013.* The Huffington Post.

Gorman, R. (2013). *Ex-Tyco Execs-Dennis Kozlowski released from prison after over eight years behind bars.* www.dailymail.co.uk.

Grey, B. (2008). *Wall Street's Great Heist of 2008.* www.wsws.org.

Grossman, A., Rexrode, C., & Fitzpatrick, D. (2014). *Bank of America Near $16 Billion to $17 Billion Settlement.* Wall Street Journal.

Hamm, T. (2014). *A Dose of Financial Reality.* The Simple Dollar.

Hanauer, N. (2014). *The Pitchforks are Coming for Us Plutocrats.* www.Politico.com.

Harkinson, J. (2011). *Michael Dell: The Making of an American Oligarch, How a homegrown geek outsourced, downsized, and tax-breaked his way to the top.* www.motherjones.com.

Hazlitt, H. (1946). *Economics in One Lesson.* Crown Publishing.

Hiltzik, M. (2012). *Poor management, not union intransigence, killed Hostess.* www.article.latimes.com.

Hiltzik, M. (2015). *IBM redefines failure as 'success,' gives underachieving CEO huge raise.* www.latimes.com.

Hungerford, T. (2012). *Taxes and the Economy: An Economic Analysis of the Top Tax Rates Since 1945.* Congressional Research service.

Ingraham, C. (2014). *Child Poverty in US is Among the Worst in the Developed World.* Washington Post.

Jacobs, H. (2015). *Here's The Ridiculous Loot That's Been Found With Corrupt Chinese Officials.* www.businessinsider.com.

Johnson, D. C. (2011). *9 Things The Rich Don't Want You To Know About Taxes.* www.wweek.com.

Johnson, R. (2013). *What Occupy Wall Street SHOULD Have Said.* www.economyandmarkets.com.

Johnson, R. (2014). *Getting an $80 Million Salary to Not Work.* economyandmarkets.

Johnston, D. C. (2003). *Perfectly Legal, The Covert Campaign to Rig our Tax system to benefit the super rich, and Cheat Everybody Else.* Penguin Group.

Johnston, D. C. (2011b). *Beyond the 1 percent.* Rueters.

Johnston, D. C. (2011c). *License to Profit: Legalized Corruption in the US Congress.* True-out.org.

Jones, M. (2013). *The Purpose of Business.* www.economicscenter.org.

King, G. (2013). *The Rise and Fall of Nikola Tesla.* www.smithsonianmag.com.

Kristoff, K. (2009). *How CEOs steal from your 401(k),* . law.harvard.edu.

Krugman, P. (2013). *Rich Man's Recovery.* New York Times.

Krugman, P. (2014). *Review of Capital in the Twenty-First Century - by Thomas Piketty, translated*

References

from the French by Arthur Goldhammer. Harvard University Press.

Krugman, P. (2014). *Why We Are Living in a New Gilded Age.* www.nybook.com.

Krugman, P. (2015). *Dewey, Cheatum and Howe.* New York Times.

Krugman, P. (2015). *Republicans against Retirement.* New York Times.

Lachman, R. (2014). *Hegemons, Empires,and their Elites.* www.SPP.Revues.org.

LaMonica, P. (2005). *Fiorina out, HP stock soars.* Money.CNN.com.

Lemco, T. (2015). *Why Pro Athletes Deserve The Money They Make.* www.sport.cbslocal.com.

Lerman, R., & Schmidt, S. (1999). *An Overview Of Economic, Social, And Demographic Trends Affecting The Us Labor Market.* the Urban Institute.

Liberto, J. (2012). *CEO pay is 380 times average worker's – AFL-CIO,.* CNN.com.

Litchenfield, M. (2015). *Why Stock Buybacks Are Bad for Investors.* www.investmentu.com.

Lomax, A. (2014). *Is Shareholder "Say on Pay" Working?* www.seattlepi.com.

Maccoby, M. (2003). *The Productive Narcissist: The Promise and Perils of Visionary Leadership.* Broadway Books.

Matthews, D. (2013). *The U.S. has a $7.25 minimum wage. Australia's is $16.88.* washingtonPost.

McClosky, D. N. (2006). *The Bourgeois Virtues: Ethics of the Age of Commerce.* University of Chicago Press.

McClosky, D. N. (2010). *The Bourgeois Dignity: Why Economists Can't Explain the Modern World.* University of Chicago Press.

Milhiser, I. (2013). *Supreme Court Rules in Favor of America's Top Lobbying Group in 13 of 16 Cases.* www.thinkprogress.org.

Miller, D. (2014). *Why Seattles's Minimum Wage Hike Matters to Seniors.* Casey Reserch.

Miller, K., Madland, D., & Weller, C. (2015). *The Reality of the Retirement Crisis.* AmericanProgress.

Mishel, L., & Davis, A. (2015). *Top CEOs Make 300 Times More than Typical Workers.* www.epi.org.

Mitchell, D. (2014). *The Economics of Creative Destruction.* danieljmitchell.wordpress.com.

Morgenson, G. (2015). *Despite Federal Regulation, C.E.O.-Worker Pay Gap Data Remains Hidden.* www.nytimes.com.

Nader, R. (2013). *The Cruel Gap Between CEO Pay and the Stagnant Minimum Wage.* www.huffingtonpost.com.

Newman, R. (2014). *Middle Class: Even Worse off Than You Thought.* www. realclearmarkets. com.

Noor, J. (2013). *Australia has $16 Minimum Wage and is the Only Rich Country to Dodge the Global Recession.* www.realnews.com.

Norris, F. (2007). *Maybe It's Time to Restructure Executive Stock Options.* New York Times.

References

Payne, J. (2011). *Off the Top of My Head- Not all Pirates are in Somalia, Environment and Economics.* www.WorldPress.com.

Pearce, D. (2012). *OVERLOOKED AND UNDERCOUNTED How the Great Recession Impacted Household Self-Sufficiency in Pennsylvania.* www.selfsufficiencystandard.org.

Perkins, T. (2014). *Progressive Kristallnacht Coming?* Wall Stereet Journal.

Piketty, T. (2014). *Capital in the 21st Century,.* Havard University Press.

Pizzigati, S. (2007). *CEOs retire with more, workers get less.* articles.sun sentinal.com.

Pizzigatti, S. (2011). *The 10 Greediest Americans of 2011.* www.nationofchange.org.

Public Citizens Congressional Watch. (2005). *Congressional Revolving Doors: The Journey from Congress to K Street.*

Reich, R. (2011). *The Limping Middle Class.* New York Times.

Rojo, J., Klinger, S., & Anderson, S. (2013). *Corporate Tax Dodgers: 10 Companies and Their Tax Loopholes.* Institute For Policy Studies.

Romero, F. (2010). *Top 10 Worst Bosses, Leona Helmsley.* www.content.time.com.

Romero, S., & Holusa, J. (2006). *Exxon Mobil Posts Largest Annual Profit for U.S. Company.* New York Times.

Rooks, A. (2012). *Job One? Selling Jobs.* ctemag.com.

Rosenbush, S. (2007). *The Analyst Who Rocked Citi, .*
        Bloomberg.

Ross, B., & Gomstyn, A. (2008). *Lehman Brothers
        Boss Defends $484 Million in Salary, Bonus.*
        abcnews.go.com.

Ruitenberg, R. (2013). *France's Hollande Gets Court
        Approval for 75% Millionaire Tax.*
        Bloomberg.

Samurai, F. (2015). *The Average Savings Rates By
        Income (Wealth Class).* financialsamurai.

Sayare, S. (2012). *Actor Renounces His Citizenship in
        Snit Over French Tax Burden.*

Schlesinger, R. (2011). *The Origins of That
        Eisenhower 'Every Gun That Is Made.*
        www.usnews.com.

Schmitt, J. (2013). *The minimum Wage is too damn
        low.* www.cepr.net.

Sherk, J. (2013). *What is Minimum Wage: Its History
        and Effects on the Economy.*
        www.heritage.org.

Sill, B. R. (2015). *Inflation, Good or Bad?* Lulu
        Publishing.

Simkins, J. (2014). *Proof: The More CEOs Make, The
        Worse Their Company Does.*
        www.outsider.com.

Sklar, H. (2004). *Outsource CEOs, not workers.*
        www.Cjonline.com.

Smith, R. (2007). *O'Neal Out as Merrill Reels From
        Loss.* Wall Street Journal.

Smith, Y. (2013). *Schadenfreude Alert: With or
        Without AIG's Help, Hank Greenberg Plans to*

References

Torture Treasury and Geithner. nakedcapitalism.

Snyder, M. (2010). *16 signs that the rich are getting richer and the poor are getting poorer*. End of the American dream.

Solman, P. (2013). *How Much Do You Need to Survive: An Interactive Guide to the Living Wage.* www.pbs.org.

Stiglitz, J. (2012). *The Price of Inequality: How Today's Divided Society Endangers Our Future.* Norton & Company.

Stockman, D. (2014). *Ben & Janet's Swell Housing Recovery: Sales Booming For The 1%; Heading Down For Everyone Else*. www.davidstockmans contracorner.com.

Stone, K. (2015). *Was Turing Pharmaceuticals 5000% price increase a tipping point?* Health News Review.

Stout, M. (2005). *The Sociopath Next Door: The Ruthless Versus the Rest of Us.* Broadway Books.

Stucke, M. (2013). *Is Competition Always Good?* Journal of Antitrust Enforcement. Oxford Journals.

Task, A. (2014). *Whining 1%-ers are wrong on moral and policy grounds.* www.finance.yahoo.com.

Thomas, F. (2012). *It's The Old Adage: Facts Don't Lie, People Do. We Get What We Deserve.* www.willblogforfood.com.

Turner, N. (2014). *Chipotle's Shareholders Slam Executive Pay at Annual Meeting.* Bloomberg.

Volsky, I. (2014). *6 Ways Extreme Income Inequality Is Making Your Life Worse.* Thinkprogress.org.

von Mises, L. (1912). *Theorie des geldes und der umlaufsmittel (The theory of money and credit).* Johnathon Cape.

White, B. (2008). *Lehman chief accepts blame for $2.8bn loss.* Financial Times.

Whitney, M. (2015). *40 Years of Economic Policy in One Chart.* www.counterpunch.org.

Widmaier, W. (2013). *Obama's pledge to raise the minimum wage is good policy.* The Conversation.

Wiggins, A., & Mathius, I. (2007). *Black Friday Revisited, the Rising Costs of "The 12 Days of XMas," a Short Play, and More!* Agora Publishing.

Williams, R. (2011). *Inside the World's Greatest Con Game.* Wall Street Daily.

Wirtz, R. (2006). *Is CEO pay too high.* Economist's View.

WorldBank. (2015). *GDP per capita in US$.* World Bank.org.

Yaccato, B. (2015). *The 13 Biggest Tax Cheats In America.* www.therichest.com.

Zinn, H. (1980). *A Peoples's History of the USA.* Harper and Row.

www.ingramcontent.com/pod-product-compliance
Lightning Source LLC
Chambersburg PA
CBHW060323200326
41519CB00011BA/1823